THE ZOO STORY

The Death
of Bessie Smith

THE SANDBOX

Three Plays, Introduced by the Author

EDWARD ALBEE

Coward, McCann & Geoghegan, Inc. New York

INTRODUCTION

With the exception of a three-act sex farce I composed when I was twelve—the action of which occurred aboard an ocean liner, the characters of which were, for the most part, English gentry, and the title of which was, for some reason that escapes me now, *Aliqueen*—with the exception of that, the three plays printed here, *The Zoo Story* (1958), and *The Death of Bessie Smith* and *The Sandbox* (both 1959), are my first three plays.

The Zoo Story, written first, received production first—but not in the United States, where one might reasonably expect an American writer to get his first attention. *The Zoo Story* had its première in Berlin, Germany, on September 28, 1959. How it got to production so shortly after it was written, and how, especially, it got to Berlin, might be of interest—perhaps to point up the Unusual, the Unlikely, the Unexpected, which, with the exception of the fare the commercial theatre setup spills out on its dogged audience each season, is the nature of the theatre.

Shortly after *The Zoo Story* was completed, and while it was being read and politely refused by a number of New York producers (which was not to be unexpected, for no one at all had ever heard of its author, and it *was* a short play, and short plays *are*, unfortunately, anathema to producers and—supposedly—to audiences), a young composer friend of mine, William Flanagan by name, looked at the play, liked it, and sent it to several friends of his, among them David Diamond, another American composer, resident in Italy; Diamond liked the play and sent it on to a friend of *his*, a Swiss actor, Pinkas Braun; Braun liked the play, made a tape recording of it, playing both its roles, which he sent on to Mrs. Stefani Hunzinger, who heads the drama department of the S. Fischer Verlag, a large publishing house in Frankfurt; she, in turn . . . well, through her it got to Berlin, and to production. From New York to Florence to Zurich to Frankfurt to Berlin. And finally back to New York where, on January 14, 1960, it received American production, off Broadway, at the Provincetown Playhouse, on a double bill with Samuel Beckett's *Krapp's Last Tape*.

I went to Berlin for the opening of *The Zoo Story*. I had not planned to—it seemed like such a distance, such an expense—but enough friends said to me that, of course, I would be present at the first performance of my first play, that I found myself, quickly enough, replying, yes, yes, of course; I wouldn't miss it for the world. And so, I went; and I *wouldn't* have missed it for the world. I wouldn't have missed it for the world, despite the fact—as I have learned since—that, for this author, at least, opening nights do not really exist. They happen, but they take place as if in a dream: One concentrates, but one cannot see the stage action clearly; one can hear but barely; one tries to follow the play, but one can make no sense of it. And, if one is called to the stage afterwards to take a bow, one wonders why, for one can make no connection between the work just presented and one's self. Naturally, this feeling was complicated in the case of *The Zoo Story*, as the play was being presented in German, a language of which I knew not a word, and in Berlin, too, an awesome city. But, it has held true since. The high points of a person's life can be appreciated so often only in retrospect.

The Death of Bessie Smith also had its première in Berlin, while *The Sandbox* was done first in New York.

The Sandbox, which is fourteen minutes long, was written to satisfy a commission from the Festival of Two Worlds for a short dramatic piece for the Festival's summer program in Spoleto, Italy—where it was not performed. I was, at the time of the commission, at work on a rather longer play, *The American Dream*, which I subsequently put aside and have, at this writing, just taken up again. For *The Sandbox,* I extracted several of the characters from *The American Dream* and placed them in a situation different than, but related to, their predicament in the longer play. They seem happy out of doors, in *The Sandbox,* and I hope they will not be distressed back in a stuffy apartment, in *The American Dream.*

Along with *The American Dream,* I am at various stages of writing, or thinking about, three other plays: two other less-than-full-evening ones—*Bedlam* and *The Substitute Speaker* (this a working title)—and a full-evening play, *The Exorcism,* or: *Who's Afraid of Virginia Woolf.*

Careers are funny things. They begin mysteriously and, just as mysteriously, they can end; and I am at just the very beginning of what I hope will be a long and satisfying life in the theatre. But, whatever happens, I am grateful to have had my novice work received so well, and so soon. And I am very happy to have these first three plays collected here.

EDWARD ALBEE

New York City
July 1, 1960

The Zoo Story

A PLAY IN ONE SCENE (1958)

For William Flanagan

FIRST PERFORMANCE: September 28, 1959. Berlin, Germany

Schiller Theater Werkstatt.

FIRST AMERICAN PERFORMANCE: January 14, 1960.
New York City.

The Provincetown Playhouse.

The Zoo Story

The Players:

PETER: A man in his early forties, neither fat nor gaunt, neither handsome nor homely. He wears tweeds, smokes a pipe, carries horn-rimmed glasses. Although he is moving into middle age, his dress and his manner would suggest a man younger.

JERRY: A man in his late thirties, not poorly dressed, but carelessly. What was once a trim and lightly muscled body has begun to go to fat; and while he is no longer handsome, it is evident that he once was. His fall from physical grace should not suggest debauchery; he has, to come closest to it, a great weariness.

The Scene:

It is Central Park; a Sunday afternoon in summer; the present. There are two park benches, one toward either side of the stage; they both face the audience. Behind them: foliage, trees, sky. At the beginning, Peter is seated on one of the benches.

Stage Directions:
> *As the curtain rises,* PETER *is seated on the bench stage-right. He is reading a book. He stops reading, cleans his glasses, goes back to reading.* JERRY *enters.*

JERRY

I've been to the zoo. (PETER *doesn't notice*) I said, I've been to the zoo. MISTER, I'VE BEEN TO THE ZOO!

PETER

Hm? . . . What? . . . I'm sorry, were you talking to me?

JERRY

I went to the zoo, and then I walked until I came here. Have I been walking north?

PETER (*Puzzled*)

North? Why . . . I . . . I think so. Let me see.

JERRY

(*Pointing past the audience*) Is that Fifth Avenue?

PETER

Why yes; yes, it is.

JERRY

And what is that cross street there; that one, to the right?

PETER

That? Oh, that's Seventy-fourth Street.

JERRY

And the zoo is around Sixty-fifth Street; so, I've been walking north.

PETER

(*Anxious to get back to his reading*) Yes; it would seem so.

JERRY

Good old north.

PETER

(*Lightly, by reflex*) Ha, ha.

JERRY

(*After a slight pause*) But not due north.

PETER

I . . . well, no, not due north; but, we . . . call it north. It's northerly.

JERRY

(*Watches as* PETER, *anxious to dismiss him, prepares his pipe*) Well, boy; *you're* not going to get lung cancer, are you?

13

PETER

(*Looks up, a little annoyed, then smiles*) No, sir. Not from this.

JERRY

No, sir. What you'll probably get is cancer of the mouth, and then you'll have to wear one of those things Freud wore after they took one whole side of his jaw away. What do they call those things?

PETER (*Uncomfortable*)

A prosthesis?

JERRY

The very thing! A prosthesis. You're an educated man, aren't you? Are you a doctor?

PETER

Oh, no; no. I read about it somewhere; *Time* magazine, I think. (*He turns to his book*)

JERRY

Well, *Time* magazine isn't for blockheads.

PETER

No, I suppose not.

JERRY

(*After a pause*) Boy, I'm glad that's Fifth Avenue there.

PETER *(Vaguely)*
Yes.

JERRY
I don't like the west side of the park much.

PETER
Oh? *(Then, slightly wary, but interested)* Why?

JERRY *(Offhand)*
I don't know.

PETER
Oh. *(He returns to his book)*

JERRY
(He stands for a few seconds, looking at PETER, *who finally looks up again, puzzled)* Do you mind if we talk?

PETER
(Obviously minding) Why . . . no, no.

JERRY
Yes you do; you do.

PETER
(Puts his book down, his pipe out and away, smiling) No, really; I don't mind.

JERRY

Yes you do.

PETER

(*Finally decided*) No; I don't mind at all, really.

JERRY

It's . . . it's a nice day.

PETER

(*Stares unnecessarily at the sky*) Yes. Yes, it is; lovely.

JERRY

I've been to the zoo.

PETER

Yes, I think you said so . . . didn't you?

JERRY

You'll read about it in the papers tomorrow, if you don't
see it on your TV tonight. You have TV, haven't you?

PETER

Why yes, we have two; one for the children.

JERRY

You're married!

16

PETER

(*With pleased emphasis*) Why, certainly.

JERRY

It isn't a law, for God's sake.

PETER

No . . . no, of course not.

JERRY

And you have a wife.

PETER

(*Bewildered by the seeming lack of communication*) Yes!

JERRY

And you have children.

PETER

Yes; two.

JERRY

Boys?

PETER

No, girls . . . both girls.

JERRY

But you wanted boys.

17

PETER

Well . . . naturally, every man wants a son, but . . .

JERRY

(*Lightly mocking*) But that's the way the cookie crumbles?

PETER (*Annoyed*)

I wasn't going to say that.

JERRY

And you're not going to have any more kids, are you?

PETER

(*A bit distantly*) No. No more. (*Then back, and irksome*) Why did you say that? How would you know about that?

JERRY

The way you cross your legs, perhaps; something in the voice. Or maybe I'm just guessing. Is it your wife?

PETER (*Furious*)

That's none of your business! (*A silence*) Do you understand? (JERRY *nods.* PETER *is quiet now*) Well, you're right. We'll have no more children.

JERRY (*Softly*)

That *is* the way the cookie crumbles.

PETER (*Forgiving*)
Yes . . . I guess so.

JERRY
Well, now; what else?

PETER
What were you saying about the zoo . . . that I'd read about it, or see . . . ?

JERRY
I'll tell you about it, soon. Do you mind if I ask you questions?

PETER
Oh, not really.

JERRY
I'll tell you why I do it; I don't talk to many people—except to say like: give me a beer, or where's the john, or what time does the feature go on, or keep your hands to yourself, buddy. You know—things like that.

PETER
I must say I don't . . .

JERRY
But every once in a while I like to talk to somebody, really *talk*; like to get to know somebody, know all about him.

PETER

(*Lightly laughing, still a little uncomfortable*) And am I the guinea pig for today?

JERRY

On a sun-drenched Sunday afternoon like this? Who better than a nice married man with two daughters and . . . uh . . . a dog? (PETER *shakes his head*) No? Two dogs. (PETER *shakes his head again*) Hm. No dogs? (PETER *shakes his head, sadly*) Oh, that's a shame. But you look like an animal man. CATS? (PETER *nods his head, ruefully*) Cats! But, that can't be your idea. No, sir. Your wife and daughters? (PETER *nods his head*) Is there anything else I should know?

PETER

(*He has to clear his throat*) There are . . . there are two parakeets. One . . . uh . . . one for each of my daughters.

JERRY

Birds.

PETER

My daughters keep them in a cage in their bedroom.

JERRY

Do they carry disease? The birds.

20

PETER

I don't believe so.

JERRY

That's too bad. If they did you could set them loose in the house and the cats could eat them and die, maybe. (PETER *looks blank for a moment, then laughs*) And what else? What do you do to support your enormous household?

PETER

I . . . uh . . . I have an executive position with a . . . a small publishing house. We . . . uh . . . we publish textbooks.

JERRY

That sounds nice; very nice. What do you make?

PETER (*Still cheerful*)

Now look here!

JERRY

Oh, come on.

PETER

Well, I make around eighteen thousand a year, but I don't carry more than forty dollars at any one time . . . in case you're a . . . a holdup man . . . ha, ha, ha.

21

JERRY

(*Ignoring the above*) Where do you live? (PETER *is reluctant*) Oh, look; I'm not going to rob you, and I'm not going to kidnap your parakeets, your cats, or your daughters.

PETER (*Too loud*)

I live between Lexington and Third Avenue, on Seventy-fourth Street.

JERRY

That wasn't so hard, was it?

PETER

I didn't mean to seem . . . ah . . . it's that you don't really carry on a conversation; you just ask questions. And I'm . . . I'm normally . . . uh . . . reticent. Why do you just stand there?

JERRY

I'll start walking around in a little while, and eventually I'll sit down. (*Recalling*) Wait until you see the expression on his face.

PETER

What? Whose face? Look here; is this something about the zoo?

22

JERRY (*Distantly*)

The what?

PETER

The zoo; the zoo. Something about the zoo.

JERRY

The zoo?

PETER

You've mentioned it several times.

JERRY

(*Still distant, but returning abruptly*) The zoo? Oh, yes; the zoo. I was there before I came here. I told you that. Say, what's the dividing line between upper-middle-middle-class and lower-upper-middle-class?

PETER

My dear fellow, I . . .

JERRY

Don't my dear fellow me.

PETER (*Unhappily*)

Was I patronizing? I believe I was; I'm sorry. But, you see, your question about the classes bewildered me.

23

JERRY

And when you're bewildered you become patronizing?

PETER

I . . . I don't express myself too well, sometimes. (*He attempts a joke on himself*) I'm in publishing, not writing.

JERRY

(*Amused, but not at the humor*) So be it. The truth *is:* *I* was being patronizing.

PETER

Oh, now; you needn't say that.
(*It is at this point that Jerry may begin to move about the stage with slowly increasing determination and authority, but pacing himself, so that the long speech about the dog comes at the high point of the arc*)

JERRY

All right. Who are your favorite writers? Baudelaire and J. P. Marquand?

PETER (*Wary*)

Well, I like a great many writers; I have a considerable . . . catholicity of taste, if I may say so. Those two men are fine, each in his way. (*Warming up*) Baudelaire, of course . . . uh . . . is by far the finer of the two, but Marquand has a place . . . in our . . . uh . . . national . . .

JERRY

Skip it.

PETER

I . . . sorry.

JERRY

Do you know what I did before I went to the zoo today? I walked all the way up Fifth Avenue from Washington Square; all the way.

PETER

Oh; you live in the Village! (*This seems to enlighten* PETER)

JERRY

No, I don't. I took the subway down to the Village so I could walk all the way up Fifth Avenue to the zoo. It's one of those things a person has to do; sometimes a person has to go a very long distance out of his way to come back a short distance correctly.

PETER (*Almost pouting*)

Oh, I thought you lived in the Village.

JERRY

What were you trying to do? Make sense out of things? Bring order? The old pigeonhole bit? Well, that's easy; I'll tell you. I live in a four-story brownstone rooming-

25

house on the upper West Side between Columbus Avenue and Central Park West. I live on the top floor; rear; west. It's a laughably small room, and one of my walls is made of beaverboard; this beaverboard separates my room from another laughably small room, so I assume that the two rooms were once one room, a small room, but not necessarily laughable. The room beyond my beaverboard wall is occupied by a colored queen who always keeps his door open; well, not always but *always* when he's plucking his eyebrows, which he does with Buddhist concentration. This colored queen has rotten teeth, which is rare, and he has a Japanese kimono, which is also pretty rare; and he wears this kimono to and from the john in the hall, which is pretty frequent. I mean, he goes to the john a lot. He never bothers me, and he never brings anyone up to his room. All he does is pluck his eyebrows, wear his kimono and go to the john. Now, the two front rooms on my floor are a little larger, I guess; but they're pretty small, too. There's a Puerto Rican family in one of them, a husband, a wife, and some kids; I don't know how many. These people entertain a lot. And in the other front room, there's somebody living there, but I don't know who it is. I've never seen who it is. Never. Never ever.

PETER (*Embarrassed*)
Why . . . why do you live there?

JERRY
(*From a distance again*) I don't know.

26

PETER

It doesn't sound like a very nice place . . . where you live.

JERRY

Well, no; it isn't an apartment in the East Seventies. But, then again, I don't have one wife, two daughters, two cats and two parakeets. What I do have, I have toilet articles, a few clothes, a hot plate that I'm not supposed to have, a can opener, one that works with a key, you know; a knife, two forks, and two spoons, one small, one large; three plates, a cup, a saucer, a drinking glass, two picture frames, both empty, eight or nine books, a pack of pornographic playing cards, regular deck, an old Western Union typewriter that prints nothing but capital letters, and a small strongbox without a lock which has in it . . . what? Rocks! Some rocks . . . sea-rounded rocks I picked up on the beach when I was a kid. Under which . . . weighed down . . . are some letters . . . please letters . . . please why don't you do this, and please when will you do that letters. And when letters, too. When will you write? When will you come? When? These letters are from more recent years.

PETER

(*Stares glumly at his shoes, then*) About those two empty picture frames . . . ?

JERRY

I don't see why they need any explanation at all. Isn't it clear? I don't have pictures of anyone to put in them.

27

PETER

Your parents . . . perhaps . . . a girl friend . . .

JERRY

You're a very sweet man, and you're possessed of a truly enviable innocence. But good old Mom and good old Pop are dead . . . you know? . . . I'm broken up about it, too . . . I mean really. BUT. That particular vaudeville act is playing the cloud circuit now, so I don't see how I can look at them, all neat and framed. Besides, or, rather, to be pointed about it, good old Mom walked out on good old Pop when I was ten and a half years old; she embarked on an adulterous turn of our southern states . . . a journey of a year's duration . . . and her most constant companion . . . among others, among many others . . . was a Mr. Barleycorn. At least, that's what good old Pop told me after he went down . . . came back . . . brought her body north. We'd received the news between Christmas and New Year's, you see, that good old Mom had parted with the ghost in some dump in Alabama. And, without the ghost . . . she was less welcome. I mean, what was she? A stiff . . . a northern stiff. At any rate, good old Pop celebrated the New Year for an even two weeks and then slapped into the front of a somewhat moving city omnibus, which sort of cleaned things out family-wise. Well no; then there was Mom's sister, who was given neither to sin nor the consolations of the bottle. I moved in on her, and my memory of her is slight excepting I remember still that she did all things dourly: sleeping, eating, working, praying. She dropped dead on the stairs to her apartment, my apartment then, too, on the afternoon of my high school graduation. A terribly middle-European joke, if you ask me.

PETER

Oh, my; oh, my.

JERRY

Oh, your what? But that was a long time ago, and I have no feeling about any of it that I care to admit to myself. Perhaps you can see, though, why good old Mom and good old Pop are frameless. What's your name? Your first name?

PETER

I'm Peter.

JERRY

I'd forgotten to ask you. I'm Jerry.

PETER

(*With a slight, nervous laugh*) Hello, Jerry.

JERRY

(*Nods his hello*) And let's see now; what's the point of having a girl's picture, especially in two frames? I have two picture frames, you remember. I never see the pretty little ladies more than once, and most of them wouldn't be caught in the same room with a camera. It's odd, and I wonder if it's sad.

PETER

The girls?

JERRY

No. I wonder if it's sad that I never see the little ladies more than once. I've never been able to have sex with, or, how is it put? . . . make love to anybody more than once. Once; that's it. . . . Oh, wait; for a week and a half, when I was fifteen . . . and I hang my head in shame that puberty was late . . . I was a h-o-m-o-s-e-x-u-a-l. I mean, I was queer . . . (*Very fast*) . . . queer, queer, queer . . . with bells ringing, banners snapping in the wind. And for those eleven days, I met at least twice a day with the park superintendent's son . . . a Greek boy, whose birthday was the same as mine, except he was a year older. I think I was very much in love . . . maybe just with sex. But that was the jazz of a very special hotel, wasn't it? And now; oh, do I love the little ladies; really, I love them. For about an hour.

PETER

Well, it seems perfectly simple to me. . . .

JERRY (*Angry*)

Look! Are you going to tell me to get married and have parakeets?

PETER (*Angry himself*)

Forget the parakeets! And stay single if you want to. It's no business of mine. I didn't start this conversation in the . . .

JERRY

All right, all right. I'm sorry. All right? You're not angry?

PETER (*Laughing*)

No, I'm not angry.

JERRY (*Relieved*)

Good. (*Now back to his previous tone*) Interesting that you asked me about the picture frames. I would have thought that you would have asked me about the pornographic playing cards.

PETER

(*With a knowing smile*) Oh, I've seen those cards.

JERRY

That's not the point. (*Laughs*) I suppose when you were a kid you and your pals passed them around, or you had a pack of your own.

PETER

Well, I guess a lot of us did.

JERRY

And you threw them away just before you got married.

PETER

Oh, now; look here. I didn't *need* anything like that when I got older.

JERRY

No?

PETER (*Embarrassed*)

I'd rather not talk about these things.

JERRY

So? Don't. Besides, I wasn't trying to plumb your post-adolescent sexual life and hard times; what I wanted to get at is the value difference between pornographic playing cards when you're a kid, and pornographic playing cards when you're older. It's that when you're a kid you use the cards as a substitute for a real experience, and when you're older you use real experience as a substitute for the fantasy. But I imagine you'd rather hear about what happened at the zoo.

PETER (*Enthusiastic*)

Oh, yes; the zoo. (*Then, awkward*) That is . . . if you. . . .

JERRY

Let me tell you about why I went . . . well, let me tell you some things. I've told you about the fourth floor of the roominghouse where I live. I think the rooms are better as you go down, floor by floor. I guess they are; I don't know. I don't know any of the people on the third and second floors. Oh, wait! I do know that there's a lady living on the third floor, in the front. I know because she cries all the time. Whenever I go out or come back in, whenever I pass her door, I always hear her crying, muffled, but . . . very determined. Very determined indeed. But the one I'm getting to, and all about the dog, is the landlady. I don't like to use words that are too harsh in describing people. I don't like to. But the landlady is a fat, ugly, mean, stupid, unwashed, misanthropic, cheap, drunken bag of garbage. And you may have noticed that I very seldom use profanity, so I can't describe her as well as I might.

PETER

You describe her . . . vividly.

JERRY

Well, thanks. Anyway, she has a dog, and I will tell you about the dog, and she and her dog are the gatekeepers of my dwelling. The woman is bad enough; she leans around in the entrance hall, spying to see that I don't bring in things or people, and when she's had her midafternoon pint of lemon-flavored gin she always stops me in the hall, and grabs ahold of my coat or my arm, and she presses her disgusting body up against me to keep me in a corner so she can talk to me. The smell of her body and her breath . . . you can't imagine it . . . and somewhere, somewhere in the back of that pea-sized brain of hers, an organ developed just enough to let her eat, drink, and emit, she has some foul parody of sexual desire. And I, Peter, I am the object of her sweaty lust.

33

PETER

That's disgusting. That's . . . horrible.

JERRY

But I have found a way to keep her off. When she talks to me, when she presses herself to my body and mumbles about her room and how I should come there, I merely say: but, Love; wasn't yesterday enough for you, and the day before? Then she puzzles, she makes slits of her tiny eyes, she sways a little, and then, Peter . . . and it is at this moment that I think I might be doing some good in that tormented house . . . a simple-minded smile begins to form on her unthinkable face, and she giggles and groans as she thinks about yesterday and the day before; as she believes and relives what never happened. Then, she motions to that black monster of a dog she has, and she goes back to her room. And I am safe until our next meeting.

PETER

It's so . . . unthinkable. I find it hard to believe that people such as that really *are*.

JERRY

(*Lightly mocking*) It's for reading about, isn't it?

PETER (*Seriously*)

Yes.

34

JERRY

And fact is better left to fiction. You're right, Peter. Well, what I have been meaning to tell you about is the dog; I shall, now.

PETER (*Nervously*)

Oh, yes; the dog.

JERRY

Don't go. You're not thinking of going, are you?

PETER

Well . . . no, I don't think so.

JERRY

(*As if to a child*) Because after I tell you about the dog, do you know what then? Then . . . then I'll tell you about what happened at the zoo.

PETER (*Laughing faintly*)

You're . . . you're full of stories, aren't you?

JERRY

You don't *have* to listen. Nobody is holding you here; remember that. Keep that in your mind.

PETER (*Irritably*)

I know that.

JERRY

You do? Good.

(The following long speech, it seems to me, should be done with a great deal of action, to achieve a hypnotic effect on Peter, and on the audience, too. Some specific actions have been suggested, but the director and the actor playing Jerry might best work it out for themselves)

ALL RIGHT. *(As if reading from a huge billboard)* THE STORY OF JERRY AND THE DOG! *(Natural again)* What I am going to tell you has something to do with how sometimes it's necessary to go a long distance out of the way in order to come back a short distance correctly; or, maybe I only think that it has something to do with that. But, it's why I went to the zoo today, and why I walked north . . . northerly, rather . . . until I came here. All right. The dog, I think I told you, is a black monster of a beast: an oversized head, tiny, tiny ears, and eyes . . . bloodshot, infected, maybe; and a body you can see the ribs through the skin. The dog is black, all black; all black except for the bloodshot eyes, and . . . yes . . . and an open sore on its . . . *right* forepaw; that is red, too. And, oh yes; the poor monster, and I do believe it's an old dog . . . it's certainly a misused one . . . almost always has an erection . . . of sorts. That's red, too. And . . . what else? . . . oh, yes; there's a gray-yellow-white color, too, when he bares his fangs. Like this: Grrrrrrr! Which is what he did when he saw me for the first time . . . the day I moved in. I worried about that animal the very first minute

36

I met him. Now, animals don't take to me like Saint Francis had birds hanging off him all the time. What I mean is: animals are indifferent to me . . . like people (*He smiles slightly*) . . . most of the time. But this dog wasn't indifferent. From the very beginning he'd snarl and then go for me, to get one of my legs. Not like he was rabid, you know; he was sort of a stumbly dog, but he wasn't half-assed, either. It was a good, stumbly run; but I always got away. He got a piece of my trouser leg, look, you can see right here, where it's mended; he got that the second day I lived there; but, I kicked free and got upstairs fast, so that was that. (*Puzzles*) I still don't know to this day how the other roomers manage it, but you know what I *think:* I think it had to do only with me. Cozy. So. Anyway, this went on for over a week, whenever I came in; but never when I went out. That's funny. Or, it *was* funny. I could pack up and live in the street for all the dog cared. Well, I thought about it up in my room one day, one of the times after I'd bolted upstairs, and I made up my mind. I decided: First, I'll kill the dog with kindness, and if that doesn't work . . . I'll just kill him. (PETER *winces*) Don't react, Peter; just listen. So, the next day I went out and bought a bag of hamburgers, medium rare, no catsup, no onion; and on the way home I threw away all the rolls and kept just the meat.

(*Action for the following, perhaps*)

When I got back to the roominghouse the dog was waiting for me. I half opened the door that led into the entrance hall, and there he was; waiting for me. It figured. I went in, very cautiously, and I had the hamburgers, you remember;

I opened the bag, and I set the meat down about twelve feet from where the dog was snarling at me. Like so! He snarled; stopped snarling; sniffed; moved slowly; then faster; then faster toward the meat. Well, when he got to it he stopped, and he looked at me. I smiled; but tentatively, you understand. He turned his face back to the hamburgers, smelled, sniffed some more, and then . . . RRRAAAAGGGGGHHHH, like that . . . he tore into them. It was as if he had never eaten anything in his life before, except like garbage. Which might very well have been the truth. I don't think the landlady ever eats anything but garbage. But. He ate all the hamburgers, almost all at once, making sounds in his throat like a woman. *Then*, when he'd finished the meat, the hamburger, and tried to eat the paper, too, he sat down and smiled. I think he smiled; I know cats do. It was a very gratifying few moments. Then, BAM, he snarled and made for me again. He didn't get me this time, either. So, I got upstairs, and I lay down on my bed and started to think about the dog again. To be truthful, I was offended, and I was damn mad, too. It was six perfectly good hamburgers with not enough pork in them to make it disgusting. I was offended. But, after a while, I decided to try it for a few more days. If you think about it, this dog had what amounted to an antipathy toward me; really. And, I wondered if I mightn't overcome this antipathy. So, I tried it for five more days, but it was always the same: snarl, sniff; move; faster; stare; gobble; RAAGGGHHH; smile; snarl; BAM. Well, now; by this time Columbus Avenue was strewn with hamburger rolls and I was less offended than disgusted. So, I decided to kill the dog.

(PETER *raises a hand in protest*)

Oh, don't be so alarmed, Peter; I didn't succeed. The day I tried to kill the dog I bought only one hamburger and what I thought was a murderous portion of rat poison. When I bought the hamburger I asked the man not to bother with the roll, all I wanted was the meat. I expected some reaction from him, like: we don't sell no hamburgers without rolls; or, wha' d'ya wanna do, eat it out'a ya han's? But no; he smiled benignly, wrapped up the hamburger in waxed paper, and said: A bite for ya pussy-cat? I wanted to say: No, not really; it's part of a plan to poison a dog I know. But, you can't say "a dog I know" without sounding funny; so I said, a little too loud, I'm afraid, and too formally: YES, A BITE FOR MY PUSSY-CAT. People looked up. It always happens when I try to simplify things; people look up. But that's neither hither nor thither. So. On my way back to the roominghouse, I kneaded the hamburger and the rat poison together between my hands, at that point feeling as much sadness as disgust. I opened the door to the entrance hall, and there the monster was, waiting to take the offering and then jump me. Poor bastard; he never learned that the moment he took to smile before he went for me gave me time enough to get out of range. BUT, there he was; malevolence with an erection, waiting. I put the poison patty down, moved toward the stairs and watched. The poor animal gobbled the food down as usual, smiled, which made me almost sick, and then, BAM.

But, I sprinted up the stairs, as usual, and the dog didn't get me, as usual. AND IT CAME TO PASS THAT THE BEAST WAS DEATHLY ILL. I knew this because he no longer attended me, and because the landlady sobered up. She stopped me in the hall the same evening of the attempted murder and confided the information that God had struck her puppy-dog a surely fatal blow. She had forgotten her bewildered lust, and her eyes were wide open for the first time. They looked like the dog's eyes. She sniveled and implored me to pray for the animal. I wanted to say to her: Madam, I have myself to pray for, the colored queen, the Puerto Rican family, the person in the front room whom I've never seen, the woman who cries deliberately behind her closed door, and the rest of the people in all roominghouses, everywhere; besides, Madam, I don't understand how to pray. But . . . to simplify things . . . I told her I would pray. She looked up. She said that I was a liar, and that I probably wanted the dog to die. I told her, and there was so much truth here, that I didn't want the dog to die. I didn't, and not just because I'd poisoned him. I'm afraid that I must tell you I wanted the dog to live so that I could see what our new relationship might come to.

(PETER *indicates his increasing displeasure and slowly growing antagonism*)

Please understand, Peter; that sort of thing is important. You must believe me; it *is* important. We have to know the effect of our actions. (*Another deep sigh*) Well, anyway; the dog recovered. I have no idea why, unless he was a descendant of the puppy that guarded the gates of hell or

40

some such resort. I'm not up on my mythology. (*He pronounces the word myth-o*-logy) Are you?

(PETER *sets to thinking, but* JERRY *goes on*)

At any rate, and you've missed the eight-thousand-dollar question, Peter; at any rate, the dog recovered his health and the landlady recovered her thirst, in no way altered by the bow-wow's deliverance. When I came home from a movie that was playing on Forty-second Street, a movie I'd seen, or one that was very much like one or several I'd seen, after the landlady told me puppykins was better, I was so hoping for the dog to be waiting for me. I was . . . well, how would you put it . . . enticed? . . . fascinated? . . . no, I don't think so . . . heart-shatteringly anxious, that's it; I was heart-shatteringly anxious to confront my friend again.

(PETER *reacts scoffingly*)

Yes, Peter; friend. That's the only word for it. I was heart-shatteringly et cetera to confront my doggy friend again. I came in the door and advanced, unafraid, to the center of the entrance hall. The beast was there . . . looking at me. And, you know, he looked better for his scrape with the nevermind. I stopped; I looked at him; he looked at me. I think . . . I think we stayed a long time that way . . . still, stone-statue . . . just looking at one another. I looked more into his face than he looked into mine. I mean, I can concentrate longer at looking into a dog's face than a dog can concentrate at looking into mine, or into anybody else's face, for that matter. But during that twenty seconds or two hours that we looked into each other's face, we made contact. Now, here is what I had wanted to hap-

41

pen: I loved the dog now, and I wanted him to love me. I had tried to love, and I had tried to kill, and both had been unsuccessful by themselves. I hoped . . . and I don't really know why I expected the dog to understand anything, much less my motivations . . . I hoped that the dog would understand.

(PETER *seems to be hypnotized*)

It's just . . . it's just that . . . (JERRY *is abnormally tense, now*) . . . it's just that if you can't deal with people, you have to make a start somewhere. WITH ANIMALS! (*Much faster now, and like a conspirator*) Don't you see? A person has to have some way of dealing with SOME-THING. If not with people . . . if not with people . . . SOMETHING. With a bed, with a cockroach, with a mirror . . . no, that's too hard, that's one of the last steps. With a cockroach, with a . . . with a . . . with a carpet, a roll of toilet paper . . . no, not that, either . . . that's a mirror, too; always check bleeding. You see how hard it is to find things? With a street corner, and too many lights, all colors reflecting on the oily-wet streets . . . with a wisp of smoke, a wisp . . . of smoke . . . with . . . with pornographic playing cards, with a strongbox . . . WITHOUT A LOCK . . . with love, with vomiting, with crying, with fury because the pretty little ladies aren't pretty little ladies, with making money with your body which is an act of love and I could prove it, with howling because you're alive; with God. How about that? WITH GOD WHO IS A COLORED QUEEN WHO WEARS A KIMONO AND PLUCKS HIS EYEBROWS, WHO

IS A WOMAN WHO CRIES WITH DETERMINA-
TION BEHIND HER CLOSED DOOR . . . with God
who, I'm told, turned his back on the whole thing
some time ago . . . with . . . some day, with people.
(JERRY *sighs the next word heavily*) People. With an idea; a
concept. And where better, where ever better in this humili-
ating excuse for a jail, where better to communicate one
single, simple-minded idea than in an entrance hall? Where?
It would be A START! Where better to make a beginning
. . . to understand and just possibly be understood . . . a
beginning of an understanding, than with . . .

> (*Here* JERRY *seems to fall into almost grotesque
> fatigue*)

. . . than with A DOG. Just that; a dog.

> (*Here there is a silence that might be prolonged for
> a moment or so; then* JERRY *wearily finishes his
> story*)

A dog. It seemed like a perfectly sensible idea. Man is a
dog's best friend, remember. So: the dog and I looked at
each other. I longer than the dog. And what I saw then has
been the same ever since. Whenever the dog and I see each
other we both stop where we are. We regard each other
with a mixture of sadness and suspicion, and then we feign
indifference. We walk past each other safely; we have an
understanding. It's very sad, but you'll have to admit that
it is an understanding. We had made many attempts at
contact, and we had failed. The dog has returned to garbage, and I to solitary but free passage. I have not returned.
I mean to say, I have *gained* solitary free passage, if that
much further loss can be said to be gain. I have learned that

neither kindness nor cruelty by themselves, independent of each other, creates any effect beyond themselves; and I have learned that the two combined, together, at the same time, are the teaching emotion. And what is gained is loss. And what has been the result: the dog and I have attained a compromise; more of a bargain, really. We neither love nor hurt because we do not try to reach each other. And, *was* trying to feed the dog an act of love? And, perhaps, was the dog's attempt to bite me *not* an act of love? If we can so misunderstand, well then, why have we invented the word love in the first place?

> (*There is silence.* JERRY *moves to* PETER's *bench and sits down beside him. This is the first time* JERRY *has sat down during the play*)

The Story of Jerry and the Dog: the end.

> (PETER *is silent*)

Well, Peter? (JERRY *is suddenly cheerful*) Well, Peter? Do you think I could sell that story to the *Reader's Digest* and make a couple of hundred bucks for *The Most Unforgettable Character I've Ever Met?* Huh?

> (JERRY *is animated, but* PETER *is disturbed*)

Oh, come on now, Peter; tell me what you think.

PETER (*Numb*)

I . . . I don't understand what . . . I don't think I . . . (*Now, almost tearfully*) Why did you tell me all of this?

JERRY

Why not?

44

PETER

I DON'T UNDERSTAND!

JERRY

(*Furious, but whispering*) That's a lie.

PETER

No. No, it's not.

JERRY (*Quietly*)

I tried to explain it to you as I went along. I went slowly; it all has to do with . . .

PETER

I DON'T WANT TO HEAR ANY MORE. I don't understand you, or your landlady, or her dog. . . .

JERRY

Her dog! I thought it was my . . . No. No, you're right. It *is* her dog. (*Looks at* PETER *intently, shaking his head*) I don't know what I was thinking about; of course you don't understand. (*In a monotone, wearily*) I don't live in your block; I'm not married to two parakeets, or whatever your setup is. I am a *permanent transient*, and my home is the sickening roominghouses on the West Side of New York City, which is the greatest city in the world. Amen.

45

PETER

I'm . . . I'm sorry; I didn't mean to . . .

JERRY

Forget it. I suppose you don't quite know what to make of me, eh?

PETER (*A joke*)

We get all kinds in publishing. (*Chuckles*)

JERRY

You're a funny man. (*He forces a laugh*) You know that? You're a very . . . a richly comic person.

PETER

(*Modestly, but amused*) Oh, now, not really. (*Still chuckling*)

JERRY

Peter, do I annoy you, or confuse you?

PETER (*Lightly*)

Well, I must confess that this wasn't the kind of afternoon I'd anticipated.

JERRY

You mean, I'm not the gentleman you were expecting.

46

PETER

I wasn't expecting anybody.

JERRY

No, I don't imagine you were. But I'm here, and I'm not leaving.

PETER

(*Consulting his watch*) Well, you may not be, but I must be getting home soon.

JERRY

Oh, come on; stay a while longer.

PETER

I really should get home; you see . . .

JERRY

(*Tickles* PETER'*s ribs with his fingers*) Oh, come on.

PETER

(*He is very ticklish; as* JERRY *continues to tickle him his voice becomes falsetto*)

No, I . . . OHHHHH! Don't do that. Stop, Stop. Ohhh, no, no.

JERRY

Oh, come on.

PETER

(*As* JERRY *tickles*) Oh, hee, hee, hee. I must go. I . . . hee, hee, hee. After all, stop, stop, hee, hee, hee, after all, the parakeets will be getting dinner ready soon. Hee, hee. And the cats are setting the table. Stop, stop, and, and . . . (PETER *is beside himself now*) . . . and we're having . . . hee, hee . . . uh . . . ho, ho, ho.

> (JERRY *stops tickling* PETER, *but the combination of the tickling and his own mad whimsy has* PETER *laughing almost hysterically. As his laughter continues, then subsides,* JERRY *watches him, with a curious fixed smile*)

JERRY

Peter?

PETER

Oh, ha, ha, ha, ha, ha. What? What?

JERRY

Listen, now.

PETER

Oh, ho, ho. What . . . what is it, Jerry? Oh, my.

JERRY (*Mysteriously*)

Peter, do you want to know what happened at the zoo?

48

Ah, ha, ha. The what? Oh, yes; the zoo. Oh, ho, ho. Well, I had my own zoo there for a moment with . . . hee, hee, the parakeets getting dinner ready, and the . . . ha, ha, whatever it was, the . . .

JERRY (*Calmly*)
Yes, that was very funny, Peter. I wouldn't have expected it. But do you want to hear about what happened at the zoo, or not?

PETER
Yes. Yes, by all means; tell me what happened at the zoo. Oh, my. I don't know what happened to me.

JERRY
Now I'll let you in on what happened at the zoo; but first, I should tell you why I went to the zoo. I went to the zoo to find out more about the way people exist with animals, and the way animals exist with each other, and with people too. It probably wasn't a fair test, what with everyone separated by bars from everyone else, the animals for the most part from each other, and always the people from the animals. But, if it's a zoo, that's the way it is. (*He pokes* PETER *on the arm*) Move over.

PETER (*Friendly*)
I'm sorry, haven't you enough room? (*He shifts a little*)

49

JERRY (*Smiling slightly*)

Well, all the animals are there, and all the people are there, and it's Sunday and all the children are there. (*He pokes* PETER *again*) Move over.

PETER

(*Patiently, still friendly*) All right.
    (*He moves some more, and* JERRY *has all the room he might need*)

JERRY

And it's a hot day, so all the stench is there, too, and all the balloon sellers, and all the ice cream sellers, and all the seals are barking, and all the birds are screaming. (*Pokes* PETER *harder*) Move over!

PETER

(*Beginning to be annoyed*) Look here, you have more than enough room! (*But he moves more, and is now fairly cramped at one end of the bench*)

JERRY

And I am there, and it's feeding time at the lions' house, and the lion keeper comes into the lion cage, one of the lion cages, to feed one of the lions. (*Punches* PETER *on the arm, hard*) MOVE OVER!

PETER

(*Very annoyed*) I can't move over any more, and stop hitting me. What's the matter with you?

JERRY

Do you want to hear the story? (*Punches* PETER'S *arm again*)

PETER (*Flabbergasted*)

I'm not so sure! I certainly don't want to be punched in the arm.

JERRY

(*Punches* PETER'S *arm again*) Like that?

PETER

Stop it! What's the matter with you?

JERRY

I'm crazy, you bastard.

PETER

That isn't funny.

JERRY

Listen to me, Peter. I want this bench. You go sit on the bench over there, and if you're good I'll tell you the rest of the story.

PETER (*Flustered*)

But . . . whatever for? What *is* the matter with you? Besides, I see no reason why I should give up this bench. I sit on this bench almost every Sunday afternoon, in good weather. It's secluded here; there's never anyone sitting here, so I have it all to myself.

JERRY (*Softly*)

Get off this bench, Peter; I want it.

PETER

(*Almost whining*) No.

JERRY

I said I want this bench, and I'm going to have it. Now get over there.

PETER

People can't have everything they want. You should know that; it's a rule; people can have some of the things they want, but they can't have everything.

JERRY (*Laughs*)

Imbecile! You're slow-witted!

PETER

Stop that!

JERRY

You're a vegetable! Go lie down on the ground.

PETER (*Intense*)

Now *you* listen to me. I've put up with you all afternoon.

52

JERRY

Not really.

PETER

LONG ENOUGH. I've put up with you long enough. I've listened to you because you seemed . . . well, because I thought you wanted to talk to somebody.

JERRY

You put things well; economically, and, yet . . . oh, what is the word I want to put justice to your . . . JESUS, you make me sick . . . get off here and give me my bench.

PETER

MY BENCH!

JERRY

(*Pushes* PETER *almost, but not quite, off the bench*) Get out of my sight.

PETER

(*Regaining his position*) God da . . . mn you. That's enough! I've had enough of you. I will not give up this bench; you can't have it, and that's that. Now, go away.
　　　(JERRY *snorts but does not move*)
Go away, I said.
　　　(JERRY *does not move*)
Get away from here. If you don't move on . . . you're a bum . . . that's what you are. . . . If you don't move on,

I'll get a policeman here and make you go.
(JERRY *laughs, stays*)
I warn you, I'll call a policeman.

                    JERRY (*Softly*)
You won't find a policeman around here; they're all over
on the west side of the park chasing fairies down from trees
or out of the bushes. That's all they do. That's their func-
tion. So scream your head off; it won't do you any good.

                         PETER
POLICE! I warn you, I'll have you arrested. POLICE!
(*Pause*) I said POLICE! (*Pause*) I feel ridiculous.

                         JERRY
You look ridiculous: a grown man screaming for the police
on a bright Sunday afternoon in the park with nobody
harming you. If a policeman *did* fill his quota and come
sludging over this way he'd probably take you in as a nut.

                         PETER
(*With disgust and impotence*) Great God, I just came here
to read, and now you want me to give up the bench. You're
mad.

                         JERRY
Hey, I got news for you, as they say. I'm on your precious
bench, and you're never going to have it for yourself again.

PETER (*Furious*)

Look, you; get off my bench. I don't care if it makes any sense or not. I want this bench to myself; I want you OFF IT!

JERRY (*Mocking*)

Aw . . . look who's mad.

PETER

GET OUT!

JERRY

No.

PETER

I WARN YOU!

JERRY

Do you know how ridiculous you look *now?*

PETER

(*His fury and self-consciousness have possessed him*) It doesn't matter. (*He is almost crying*) GET AWAY FROM MY BENCH!

JERRY

Why? You have everything in the world you want; you've told me about your home, and your family, and *your own* little zoo. You have everything, and now you want this bench. Are these the things men fight for? Tell me, Peter, is this bench, this iron and this wood, is this your honor? Is this the thing in the world you'd fight for? Can you think of anything more absurd?

PETER

Absurd? Look, I'm not going to talk to you about honor, or even try to explain it to you. Besides, it isn't a question of honor; but even if it were, you wouldn't understand.

JERRY (*Contemptuously*)

You don't even know what you're saying, do you? This is probably the first time in your life you've had anything more trying to face than changing your cats' toilet box. Stupid! Don't you have any idea, not even the slightest, what other people *need?*

PETER

Oh, boy, listen to you; well, you don't need this bench. That's for sure.

JERRY

Yes; yes, I do.

PETER (*Quivering*)

I've come here for years; I have hours of great pleasure, great satisfaction, right here. And that's important to a man. I'm a responsible person, and I'm a GROWNUP. This is my bench, and you have no right to take it away from me.

JERRY

Fight for it, then. Defend yourself; defend your bench.

PETER

You've *pushed* me to it. Get up and fight.

JERRY

Like a man?

PETER (*Still angry*)

Yes, like a man, if you insist on mocking me even further.

JERRY

I'll have to give you credit for one thing: you *are* a vegetable, and a slightly nearsighted one, I think . . .

PETER

THAT'S ENOUGH. . . .

JERRY

. . . but, you know, as they say on TV all the time—you know—and I mean this, Peter, you have a certain dignity; it surprises me. . . .

PETER

STOP!

JERRY

(*Rises lazily*) Very well, Peter, we'll battle for the bench, but we're not evenly matched.

> (*He takes out and clicks open an ugly-looking knife*)

PETER

> (*Suddenly awakening to the reality of the situation*) You *are* mad! You're stark raving mad! YOU'RE GOING TO KILL ME!

> (*But before* PETER *has time to think what to do,* JERRY *tosses the knife at* PETER's *feet*)

JERRY

There you go. Pick it up. You have the knife and we'll be more evenly matched.

PETER (*Horrified*)

No!

JERRY

> (*Rushes over to* PETER, *grabs him by the collar;* PETER *rises; their faces almost touch*)

Now you pick up that knife and you fight with me. You fight for your self-respect; you fight for that goddamned bench.

PETER (*Struggling*)

No! Let . . . let go of me! He . . . Help!

JERRY

(*Slaps* PETER *on each "fight"*) You fight, you miserable bastard; fight for that bench; fight for your parakeets; fight for your cats, fight for your two daughters; fight for your wife; fight for your manhood, you pathetic little vegetable. (*Spits in* PETER's *face*) You couldn't even get your wife with a male child.

PETER

(*Breaks away, enraged*) It's a matter of genetics, not manhood, you . . . you monster.
> (*He darts down, picks up the knife and backs off a little; he is breathing heavily*)

I'll give you one last chance; get out of here and leave me alone!
> (*He holds the knife with a firm arm, but far in front of him, not to attack, but to defend*)

JERRY (*Sighs heavily*)

So be it!
> (*With a rush he charges* PETER *and impales himself on the knife. Tableau: For just a moment, complete silence,* JERRY *impaled on the knife at the end of* PETER's *still firm arm. Then* PETER *screams, pulls away, leaving the knife in* JERRY. JERRY *is motionless, on point. Then he, too, screams, and it must be the sound of an infuriated and fatally wounded animal. With the knife in him, he stumbles back to*

> the bench that PETER *had vacated. He crumbles
> there, sitting, facing* PETER, *his eyes wide in agony,
> his mouth open*)

PETER (*Whispering*)

Oh my God, oh my God, oh my God. . . .
> (*He repeats these words many times, very rapidly*)

JERRY

> (JERRY *is dying; but now his expression seems to
> change. His features relax, and while his voice
> varies, sometimes wrenched with pain, for the most
> part he seems removed from his dying. He smiles*)

Thank you, Peter. I mean that, now; thank you very much.
> (PETER's *mouth drops open. He cannot move; he is
> transfixed*)

Oh, Peter, I was so afraid I'd drive you away. (*He laughs
as best he can*) You don't know how afraid I was you'd go
away and leave me. And now I'll tell you what happened
at the zoo. I think . . . I think this is what happened at the
zoo . . . I think. I think that while I was at the zoo I decided that I would walk north . . . northerly, rather . . .
until I found you . . . or somebody . . . and I decided
that I would talk to you . . . I would tell you things
. . . and things that I would tell you would . . . Well,
here we are. You see? Here we *are*. But . . . I don't know
. . . could I have planned all this? No . . . no, I couldn't
have. But I think I did. And now I've told you what you
wanted to know, haven't I? And now you know all about
what happened at the zoo. And now you know what you'll

see in your TV, and the face I told you about . . . you remember . . . the face I told you about . . . my face, the face you see right now. Peter . . . Peter? . . . Peter . . . thank you. I came unto you (*He laughs, so faintly*) and you have comforted me. Dear Peter.

PETER
(*Almost fainting*) Oh my God!

JERRY
You'd better go now. Somebody might come by, and you don't want to be here when anyone comes.

PETER
(*Does not move, but begins to weep*)
Oh my God, oh my God.

JERRY
(*Most faintly, now; he is very near death*)
You won't be coming back here any more, Peter; you've been dispossessed. You've lost your bench, but you've defended your honor. And Peter, I'll tell you something now; you're not really a vegetable; it's all right, you're an animal. You're an animal, too. But you'd better hurry now, Peter. Hurry, you'd better go . . . see?
> (JERRY *takes a handkerchief and with great effort and pain wipes the knife handle clean of finger-prints*)
Hurry away, Peter.
> (PETER *begins to stagger away*)

Wait . . . wait, Peter. Take your book . . . book. Right
here . . . beside me . . . on your bench . . . my bench,
rather. Come . . . take your book.

    (PETER *starts for the book, but retreats*)

Hurry . . . Peter.

    (PETER *rushes to the bench, grabs the book, re-
treats*)

Very good, Peter . . . very good. Now . . . hurry away.

    (PETER *hesitates for a moment, then flees, stage-
left*)

Hurry away. . . . (*His eyes are closed now*) Hurry away,
your parakeets are making the dinner . . . the cats . . .
are setting the table . . .

PETER (Off stage)

    (*A pitiful howl*)

OH MY GOD!

JERRY

    (*His eyes still closed, he shakes his head and speaks;
a combination of scornful mimicry and supplication*)

Oh . . . my . . . God.

    (*He is dead*)

CURTAIN

The Death of Bessie Smith

A PLAY IN EIGHT SCENES (1959)

For Ned Rorem

FIRST PERFORMANCE: April 21, 1960. Berlin, Germany.

Schlosspark Theater.

The Death of Bessie Smith

The Players:

BERNIE: A Negro, about forty, thin.

JACK: A dark-skinned Negro, forty-five, bulky, with a deep voice and a mustache.

THE FATHER: A thin, balding white man, about fifty-five.

THE NURSE: A southern white girl, full blown, dark or red-haired, pretty, with a wild laugh. Twenty-six.

THE ORDERLY: A light-skinned Negro, twenty-eight, clean-shaven, trim, prim.

SECOND NURSE: A southern white girl, blond, not too pretty, about thirty.

THE INTERN: A southern white man, blond, well put-to-gether, with an amiable face; thirty.

The Scene:

Afternoon and early evening, September 26, 1937. In and around the city of Memphis, Tennessee.

The Set:

The set for this play will vary, naturally, as stages vary—from theatre to theatre. So, the suggestions put down below, while they might serve as a useful guide, are but a general idea—what the author "sees."

What the author "sees" is this: The central and front area of the stage reserved for the admissions room of a hospital, for this is where the major portion of the action of the play takes place. The admissions desk and chair stage-center, facing the audience. A door, leading outside, stage-right; a door, leading to further areas of the hospital, stage-left. Very little more: a bench, perhaps; a chair or two. Running along the rear of the stage, and perhaps a bit on the sides, there should be a raised platform, on which, at various locations, against just the most minimal suggestions of sets, the other scenes of the play are performed. All of this very open, for the whole back wall of the stage is full of the sky, which will vary from scene to scene: a hot blue; a sunset; a great, red-orange-yellow sunset. Sometimes full, sometimes but a hint.

At the curtain, let the entire stage be dark against the sky, which is a hot blue. *Music* against this, for a moment or so, fading to under as the lights come up on:

SCENE ONE

The corner of a barroom. BERNIE *seated at a table, a beer before him, with glass.* JACK *enters, tentatively, a beer bottle in his hand; he does not see* BERNIE.

BERNIE

(*Recognizing* JACK; *with pleased surprise*) Hey!

JACK

Hm?

BERNIE

Hey; Jack!

JACK

Hm? . . . What? . . . (*Recognizes him*) Bernie!

BERNIE

What you doin' here, boy? C'mon, sit down.

JACK

Well, I'll be damned. . . .

BERNIE

C'mon, sit down, Jack.

JACK

Yeah . . . sure . . . well, I'll be damned. (*Moves over to the table; sits*) Bernie. My God, it's hot. How you been, boy?

BERNIE

Fine; fine. What you *doin'* here?

JACK

Oh, travelin'; travelin'.

BERNIE

On the move, hunh? Boy, you are the last person I expected t'walk in that door; small world, hunh?

JACK

Yeah; yeah.

BERNIE

On the move, hunh? Where you goin'?

JACK

(*Almost, but not quite, mysterious*) North.

BERNIE (*Laughs*)

North! North? That's a big place, friend: north.

JACK

Yeah . . . yeah, it is that: a big place.

BERNIE

(*After a pause; laughs again*) Well, *where*, boy? North *where?*

JACK

(*Coyly; proudly*) New York.

70

BERNIE

New York!

JACK

Unh-hunh; unh-hunh.

BERNIE

New York, hunh? Well. What you got goin' up there?

JACK

(*Coy again*) Oh . . . well . . . I got somethin' goin' up there. What *you* been up to, boy?

BERNIE

New York, hunh?

JACK

(*Obviously dying to tell about it*) Unh-hunh.

BERNIE

(*Knowing it*) Well, now, isn't that somethin'. Hey! You want a beer? You want another beer?

JACK

No, I gotta get . . . well, I don't know, I . . .

BERNIE

(*Rising from the table*) Sure you do. Hot like this? You need a beer or two, cool you off.

71

JACK

(*Settling back*) Yeah; why not? Sure, Bernie.

BERNIE

(*A dollar bill in his hand; moving off*) I'll get us a pair. New York, hunh? What's it all about, Jack? Hunh?

JACK (*Chuckles*)

Ah, you'd be surprised, boy; you'd be surprised.
(*Lights fade on this scene, come up on another, which is*)

SCENE TWO

Part of a screened-in porch; some wicker furniture, a little the worse for wear.
The NURSE'S FATHER *is seated on the porch, a cane by his chair. Music, loud, from a phonograph, inside.*

FATHER

(*The music is too loud; he grips the arms of his chair; finally*) Stop it! Stop it! Stop it! Stop it!

NURSE (*From inside*)

What? What did you say?

FATHER

STOP IT!

NURSE

(*Appearing, dressed for duty*) I can't hear you; what do you want?

FATHER

Turn it off! Turn that goddam music off!

NURSE

Honestly, Father . . .

FATHER

Turn it off!
> (*The* NURSE *turns wearily, goes back inside. Music stops*)

Goddam nigger records. (*To* NURSE, *inside*) I got a headache.

NURSE (*Re-entering*)

What?

FATHER

I said, I got a headache; you play those goddam records all the time; blast my head off; you play those goddam nigger records full blast . . . me with a headache. . . .

NURSE (*Wearily*)

You take your pill?

FATHER

No!

73

NURSE (*Turning*)

I'll get you your pills. . . .

FATHER

I don't want 'em!

NURSE (*Overpatiently*)

All right; then I won't get you your pills.

FATHER

(*After a pause; quietly, petulantly*) You play those goddam records all the time. . . .

NURSE (*Impatiently*)

I'm sorry, Father; I didn't know you had your headache.

FATHER

Don't you use that tone with me!

NURSE

(*With that tone*) I wasn't using any tone. . . .

FATHER

Don't argue!

NURSE

I am not arguing; I don't *want* to argue; it's too *hot* to argue. (*Pause; then quietly*) I don't see why a person can't play a couple of records around here without . . .

FATHER

Damn noise! That's all it is; damn noise.

NURSE

(*After a pause*) I don't suppose you'll drive me to work. I don't suppose, with your headache, you feel up to driving me to the hospital.

FATHER

No.

NURSE

I didn't think you would. And I suppose *you're* going to need the car, too.

FATHER

Yes.

NURSE

Yes; I figured you would. What are you going to do, Father? Are you going to sit here all afternoon on the porch, with your headache, and *watch* the car? Are you going to sit here and watch it all afternoon? You going to sit here with a shotgun and make sure the birds don't crap on it . . . or something?

FATHER

I'm going to need it.

75

NURSE

Yeah; sure.

FATHER

I said, I'm going to need it.

NURSE

Yeah . . . I heard you. You're going to need it.

FATHER

I am!

NURSE

Yeah; no doubt. You going to drive down to the Democratic Club, and sit around with that bunch of loafers? You going to play big politician today? Hunh?

FATHER

That's enough, now.

NURSE

You going to go down there with that bunch of bums . . . light up one of those expensive cigars, which you have no business smoking, which you can't afford, which *I* cannot afford, to put it more accurately . . . the same brand His Honor the mayor smokes . . . you going to sit down there and talk big, about how you and the mayor are like *this* . . . you going to pretend you're something more than you really are, which is nothing but . . .

FATHER

You be quiet, you!

NURSE

. . . a hanger-on . . . a flunky . . .

FATHER

YOU BE QUIET!

NURSE (*Faster*)

Is that what you need the car for, Father, and I am going to have to take that hot, stinking bus to the hospital?

FATHER

I said, quiet! (*Pause*) I'm sick and tired of hearing you disparage my friendship with the mayor.

NURSE (*Contemptuous*)

Friendship!

FATHER

That's right: friendship.

NURSE

I'll tell you what I'll do: Now that we have His Honor, the mayor, as a patient . . . when I get down to the hospital . . . if I ever get there on that damn bus . . . I'll pay him a call, and I'll just *ask* him about your "friendship" with him; I'll just . . .

77

FATHER

Don't you go disturbing him; you hear me?

NURSE

Why, I should think the mayor would be de*light*ed if the daughter of one of his closest friends was to . . .

FATHER

You're going to make trouble!

NURSE (*Heavily sarcastic*)

Oh, how could I make trouble, Father?

FATHER

You be careful.

NURSE

Oh, that must be quite a friendship. Hey, I got a good idea: you could drive me down to the hospital and you could pay a visit to your good friend the mayor at the same time. Now, *that* is a good idea.

FATHER

Leave off! Just leave off!

NURSE

(*Under her breath*) You make me sick.

FATHER

What! What was that?

NURSE (*Very quietly*)

I said, you make me sick, Father.

FATHER

Yeah? Yeah?
(*He takes his cane, raps it against the floor several times. This gesture, beginning in anger, alters, as it becomes weaker, to a helpless and pathetic flailing; eventually it subsides; the* NURSE *watches it all quietly*)

NURSE (*Tenderly*)

Are you done?

FATHER

Go away; go to work.

NURSE

I'll get you your pills before I go.

FATHER (*Tonelessly*)

I said, I don't want them.

NURSE

I don't care whether you *want* them, or not. . . .

FATHER

I'm not one of your patients!

NURSE

Oh, and aren't I glad you're not.

FATHER

You give them better attention than you give me!

NURSE (*Wearily*)

I don't have patients, Father; I am not a floor nurse; will you get that into your head? I am on admissions; I am on the admissions desk. You *know* that; why do you pretend otherwise?

FATHER

If you were a . . . what-do-you-call-it . . . if you were a floor nurse . . . if you *were*, you'd give your patients better attention than you give me.

NURSE

What *are* you, Father? What are you? Are you sick, or not? Are you a . . . a . . . a poor cripple, or are you planning to get yourself up out of that chair, after I go to work, and drive yourself down to the Democratic Club and sit around with that bunch of loafers? Make up your mind, Father; you can't have it every which way.

FATHER

Never mind.

NURSE

You can't; you just can't.

FATHER

Never mind, now!

NURSE

(*After a pause*) Well, I gotta get to work.

FATHER (*Sneering*)

Why don't you get your boy friend to drive you to work?

NURSE

All right; leave off.

FATHER

Why don't you get him to come by and pick you up, hunh?

NURSE

I said, leave off!

FATHER

Or is he only interested in driving you back here at night
. . . when it's nice and dark; when it's plenty dark for

81

messing around in his car? Is that it? Why don't you bring
him here and let *me* have a look at him; why don't you
let me get a look at him some time?

NURSE (*Angry*)

Well, Father . . . (*A very brief gesture at the surround-
ings*) maybe it's because I don't want him to get a . . .

FATHER

I hear you; I hear you at night; I hear you gigglin' and
carrying on out there in his car; I hear you!

NURSE

(*Loud; to cover the sound of his voice*) I'm going, Father.

FATHER

All right; get along, then; get on!

NURSE

You're damned right!

FATHER

Go on! Go!
    (*The* NURSE *regards him for a moment; turns, exits*)
And don't stay out there all night in his car, when you get
back. You hear me? (*Pause*) You hear me?
    (*Lights fade on this scene; come up on*)

SCENE THREE

A bare area. JACK *enters, addresses his remarks off
stage and to an invisible mirror on an invisible
dresser. Music under this scene, as though coming
from a distance.*

JACK

Hey . . . Bessie! C'mon, now. Hey . . . honey? Get
your butt out of bed . . . wake up. C'mon; the goddam
afternoon's half gone; we gotta get movin'. Hey . . . I
called that son-of-a-bitch in New York . . . *I* told him,
all right. I told him what you said. Wake up, baby, we
gotta get out of this dump; I gotta get you to Memphis
'fore seven o'clock . . . and then . . . POW! . . . *we*
are headin' straight north. Here we come; NEW YORK.
I told that bastard . . . I said: Look, you don't have no
exclusive rights on Bessie . . . nobody's got 'em . . .
Bessie is doin' you a favor . . . she's doin' you a goddam
favor. She don't *have* to sing for you. I said: Bessie's tired
. . . she don't wanna travel now. An' he said: You don't
wanna back out of this . . . Bessie told me *herself* . . . and
I said: Look . . . don't worry yourself . . . Bessie said
she'd cut more sides for you . . . she will . . . she'll make
all the goddam new records you want. . . . What I mean
to say *is*, just don't you get any ideas about havin' exclusive
rights . . . because nobody's got 'em. (*Giggles*) I told him
you was free as a bird, honey. Free as a goddam bird.

83

(*Looks in at her, shakes his head*) Some bird! I been down-stairs to check us out. I go downstairs to check us out, and I run into a friend of mine . . . and we sit in the bar and have a few, and he says: What're *you* doin' now; what're you doin' in this crummy hotel? And I say: I am cartin' a bird around with me. I'm cartin' her north; I got a fat lady upstairs; she is sleepin' off last night. An' he says: You always got *some* fat lady upstairs, somewhere; boy, I never seen it fail. An' I say: This ain't just no plain fat lady I got upstairs . . . this is a celebrity, boy . . . this is a rich old fat singin' lady . . . an' he laughed an' he said: Boy, who you got up there? I say: You guess. An' he says: C'mon . . . I can't *guess.* An' I told him . . . I am travelin' with Miss Bessie Smith. An' he looked at me, an' he said, real quiet: Jesus, boy, are you travelin' with Bessie? An' I said . . . an' real proud: You're damn right I'm travelin' with Bessie. An' he wants to meet you; so you get your big self out of bed; we're goin' to go downstairs, 'cause I wanna show you off. C'mon, now; I mean I *gotta* show you off. 'Cause then he said: "Whatever *happened* to Bessie? An' I said: What do you mean, whatever hap-pened to Bessie? She's right upstairs. An' he said: I mean, what's she been doin' the past four-five years? There was a time there, boy, Chicago an' all, New York, she was the hottest goddam thing goin'. Is she still singin'? YOU HEAR THAT? That's what he said: Is she still singin'? An' I said . . . I said, you been tired . . . you been restin'. You ain't been forgotten, honey, but they are askin' questions. SO YOU GET UP! We're drivin' north tonight, an' when

you get in New York . . . *you* show 'em where you been.
Honey, you're gonna go back on top again . . . I mean it
. . . you *are*. I'm gonna get you up to New York. 'Cause
you gotta make that date. I mean, sure, baby, you're free
as a goddam bird, an' I did tell that son-of-a-bitch he don't
have exclusive rights on you . . . but, honey . . . he *is*
interested . . . an' you gotta hustle for it now. You do;
'cause if you don't do *somethin'*, people are gonna stop
askin' where you been the past four-five years . . . they're
gonna stop askin' anything at all! You hear? An' if I say
downstairs you're rich . . . that don't make it so, Bessie.
No more, honey. You gotta make this goddam trip . . .
you gotta get goin' again. (*Pleading*) Baby? Honey? You
know I'm not lyin' to you. C'mon now; get up. We go
downstairs to the bar an' have a few . . . see my friend
. . . an' then we'll get in that car . . . and *go*. 'Cause it's
gettin' late, honey . . . it's gettin' awful late. (*Brighter*)
Hey! You awake? (*Moving to the wings*) Well, c'mon,
then, Bessie . . . let's get up. We're goin' north again!
  (*The lights fade on this scene.*
  Music.
  The sunset is predominant)

JACK'S VOICE

Ha, ha; thanks; thanks a lot. (*Car door slams. Car motor
starts*) O.K.; here we go; we're on our way. (*Sound of car
motor gunning, car moving off, fading*)
  (*The sunset dims again.*
  Music, fading, as the lights come up on)

SCENE FOUR

The admissions room of the hospital. The NURSE *is at her desk; the* ORDERLY *stands to one side.*

ORDERLY

The mayor of Memphis! I went into his room and there he was; the mayor of Memphis. Lying right there, flat on his belly . . . a cigar in his mouth . . . an unlit cigar stuck in his mouth, chewing on it, chewing on a big, unlit cigar . . . shuffling a lot of papers in his hands, a pillow shoved up under his chest to give him some freedom for all those papers . . . and I came in, and I said: Good afternoon, Your Honor . . . and he swung his face 'round and he looked at me and he shouted: My ass hurts, you get the hell out of here!

NURSE (*Laughs freely*)

His Honor has got his ass in a sling, and that's for sure.

ORDERLY

And I got out; I left very quickly; I closed the door fast.

NURSE

The mayor and his hemorrhoids . . . the mayor's late hemorrhoids . . . are a matter of deep concern to this institution, for the mayor built this hospital; the mayor is here with his ass in a sling, and the seat of government is now in Room 206 . . . so you be nice and respectful. (*Laughs*)

There is a man two rooms down who walked in here last night after you went off . . . that man walked in here with his hands over his gut to keep his insides from spilling right out on this desk . . .

ORDERLY

I heard. . . .

NURSE

. . . and that man may live, or he may not live, and the wagers are heavy that he will not live . . . but we are not one bit more concerned for that man than we are for His Honor . . . no sir.

ORDERLY (*Chuckling*)

I like your contempt.

NURSE

You what? You like my *contempt,* do you? Well now, don't misunderstand me. Just what do you think I meant? What have you got it in your mind that I was saying?

ORDERLY

Why, it's a matter of proportion. Surely you don't *condone* the fact that the mayor and his piles, and that poor man lying up there . . . ?

NURSE

Condone! Will you listen to that: condone! My! Aren't you the educated one? What . . . what does that word mean, boy? That word condone? Hunh? You do talk some, don't you? You have a great deal to learn. Now it's true that the poor man lying up there with his guts coming out could be a nigger for all the attention he'd get if His Honor should start shouting for something . . . he could be on the operating table . . . and they'd drop his insides right on the floor and come running if the mayor should want his cigar lit. . . . But that is the way things *are*. Those are facts. You had better acquaint yourself with some realities.

ORDERLY

I know . . . I know the mayor is an important man. He *is* impressive . . . even lying on his belly like he is. . . . I'd like to get to talk to him.

NURSE

Don't you know it! TALK to him! Talk to the mayor? What for?

ORDERLY

I've told you. I've told you I don't intend to stay here carrying crap pans and washing out the operating theatre until I have a . . . a long gray beard . . . I'm . . . I'm going beyond that.

NURSE (*Patronizing*)

Sure.

ORDERLY

I've told you . . . I'm going beyond that. This . . .

NURSE

(*Shakes her head in amused disbelief*) Oh, my. Listen . . .
you should count yourself lucky, boy. Just what do you
think is going to happen to you? Is His Honor, the mayor,
going to rise up out of his sickbed and take a personal
interest in you? Write a letter to the President, maybe?
And is Mr. Roosevelt going to send his wife, Lady Eleanor,
down here after you? Or is it in your plans that you are
going to be handed a big fat scholarship somewhere to
the north of Johns Hopkins? Boy, you just don't know!
I'll tell you something . . . you are lucky as you are.
Whatever do you expect?

ORDERLY

What's been promised. . . . Nothing more. Just that.

NURSE

Promised! Promised? Oh, boy, I'll tell you about promises.
Don't you know yet that everything is promises . . . and
that is all there is to it? Promises . . . nothing more! I am
personally sick of promises. Would you like to hear a little
poem? Would you like me to recite some verse for you?
Here is a little poem: "You kiss the niggers and I'll kiss the
Jews and we'll stay in the White House as long as we
choose." And that . . . according to what I am told . . .
that is what Mr. and Mrs. Roosevelt sit at the breakfast

table and sing to each other over their orange juice, right in the White House. Promises, boy! Promises . . . and that is what they are going to stay.

ORDERLY

There are *some* people who believe in more than promises. . . .

NURSE

Hunh?

ORDERLY (Cautious now)

I say, there are some people who believe in more than promises; there are some people who believe in action.

NURSE

What's that? What did you say?

ORDERLY

Action . . . ac— . . . Never mind.

NURSE (Her eyes narrow)

No . . . no, go on now . . . action? What kind of action do you mean?

ORDERLY

I don't *mean* anything . . . all I said was . . .

90

NURSE

I heard you. You know . . . I know what you been doing.
You been listening to the great white doctor again . . .
that big, good-looking blond intern you *admire* so much
because he is so liberal-thinking, eh? My suitor? (*Laughs*)
My suitor . . . my very own white knight, who is wast-
ing his time patching up decent folk right here when there
is dying going on in Spain. (*Exaggerated*) Oh, there is dying in Spain. And he is held here! That's who you have
been listening to.

ORDERLY

I don't mean that. . . . I don't pay any attention . . .
(*Weakly*) to that kind of talk. I do my job here . . . I try
to keep . . .

NURSE (*Contemptuous*)

You try to keep yourself on the good side of everybody,
don't you, boy? You stand there and you nod your kinky
little head and say yes'm, yes'm, at everything I say, and
then when he's here you go off in a corner and you get
him and you sympathize with him . . . you get him to
tell you about . . . promises! . . . and . . . and . . . action! . . . I'll tell you right now, he's going to get himself
into trouble . . . and you're helping him right along.

ORDERLY

No, now. I don't . . .

91

NURSE (*With some disgust*)

All that talk of his! Action! I know all what he talks about
. . . like about that bunch of radicals came through here
last spring . . . causing the rioting . . . that arson! Stuff
like that. Didn't . . . didn't you have someone get banged
up in that?

ORDERLY (*Contained*)

My uncle got run down by a lorry full of state police . . .

NURSE

. . . which the Governor called out because of the rioting
. . . and that arson! Action! That was a fine bunch of
action. Is that what you mean? Is that what you get him off
in a corner and get him to talk about . . . and pretend
you're interested? Listen, boy . . . if you're going to get
yourself in with those folks, you'd better . . .

ORDERLY (*Quickly*)

I'm not mixed up with any folks . . . honestly . . . I'm
not. I just want to . . .

NURSE

I'll tell you what you just want. . . . I'll tell you what you
just want if you have any mind to keep this good job
you've got. . . . You just shut your ears . . . and you
keep that mouth closed tight, too. All this talk about what
you are going to go beyond! You keep walking a real

tight line here, and . . . and at night . . . (*She begins to giggle*) . . . and at night, if you want to, on your own time . . . at night you keep right on putting that bleach on your hands and your neck and your face . . .

ORDERLY

I do no such thing!

NURSE (*In full laughter*)

. . . and you keep right on bleaching away . . . b-l-e-a-c-h-i-n-g a-w-a-y . . . but you do that on your own time . . . you can do all that on your own time.

ORDERLY (*Pleading*)

I do no such thing!

NURSE

The hell you don't! You are such a . . .

ORDERLY

That kind of talk is very . . .

NURSE

. . . you are so mixed up! You are going to be one funny sight. You, over there in a corner playing up to him . . . well, boy, you are going to be one funny sight come the millennium. . . . The great black mob marching down the street, banners in the air . . . that great black mob . . . and you right there in the middle, your bleached-out,

snowy-white face in the middle of the pack like that . . .
(*She breaks down in laughter*) . . . oh . . . oh, my . . .
oh. I tell you, that will be quite a sight.

ORDERLY (*Plaintive*)

I wish you'd stop that.

NURSE

Quite a sight.

ORDERLY

I wish you wouldn't make fun of me . . . I don't give **you**
any cause.

NURSE

Oh, my . . . oh, I *am* sorry . . . I am *so* sorry.

ORDERLY

I don't think I give you any cause. . . .

NURSE

You don't, eh?

ORDERLY

No.

NURSE

Well . . . you *are* a true little gentleman, that's for sure
. . . you *are* polite . . . and deferential . . . and you are

94

a genuine little ass-licker, if I ever saw one. Tell me, boy . . .

ORDERLY

(*Stiffening a little*) There is no need . . .

NURSE

(*Maliciously solicitous*) Tell me, boy . . . is it true that you have Uncle Tom'd yourself right out of the bosom of your family . . . right out of your circle of acquaintances? Is it true, young man, that you are now an inhabitant of no-man's-land, on the one side shunned and disowned by your brethren, and on the other an object of contempt and derision to your betters? Is that your problem, son?

ORDERLY

You . . . you shouldn't do that. I . . . work hard . . . I try to advance myself . . . I give nobody trouble.

NURSE

I'll tell you what you do. . . . You go north, boy . . . you go up to New York City, where nobody's any better than anybody else . . . get up north, boy. (*Abrupt change of tone*) But before you do anything like that, you run on downstairs and get me a pack of cigarettes.

ORDERLY

(*Pauses. Is about to speak; thinks better of it; moves off to door, rear*) Yes'm.
(*Exits*)

NURSE

(*Watches him leave. After he is gone, shakes her head, laughs, parodies him*)

Yes'm . . . yes'm . . . ha, ha, ha! You white niggers kill me.

(*She picks up her desk phone, dials a number, as the lights come up on*)

SCENE FIVE

Which is both the hospital set of the preceding scene and, as well, on the raised platform, another admissions desk of another hospital. The desk is empty. The phone rings, twice. The SECOND NURSE *comes in, slowly, filing her nails, maybe.*

SECOND NURSE

(*Lazily answering the phone*) Mercy Hospital.

NURSE

Mercy Hospital! Mercy, indeed, you away from your desk all the time. *Some* hospitals are run better than *others; some* nurses stay at their posts.

SECOND NURSE (*Bored*)

Oh, hi. What do you want?

NURSE

I don't *want* anything. . . .

SECOND NURSE

(*Pause*) Oh. Well, what did you call for?

NURSE

I didn't call *for* anything. I (*Shrugs*) just called.

SECOND NURSE

Oh.
> (*The lights dim a little on the two nurses.*
> *Music.*
> *Car sounds up*)

JACK'S VOICE

(*Laughs*) I tell you, honey, he didn't like that. No, sir, he didn't. You comfortable, honey. Hunh? You just lean back and enjoy the ride, baby; we're makin' good time. Yes, we are makin' . . . WATCH OUT! WATCH . . .
> (*Sound of crash. . . . Silence*)

Honey . . . baby . . . we have crashed . . . you all right? . . . BESSIE! BESSIE!
> (*Music up again, fading as the lights come up full*
> *again on the two nurses*)

NURSE

. . . and, what else? Oh, yeah; *we* have got the mayor here.

SECOND NURSE

That's nice. What's he doin'?

NURSE

He isn't *doin'* anything; he is a patient here.

SECOND NURSE

Oh. Well, *we* had the mayor's wife *here* . . . last April.

NURSE

Unh-hunh. Well, *we* got the mayor *here*, now.

SECOND NURSE (*Very bored*)

Unh-hunh. Well, that's nice.

NURSE

(*Turns, sees the* INTERN *entering*) Oh, lover-boy just walked in; I'll call you later, hunh?

SECOND NURSE

Unh-hunh.
    (*They both hang up. The lights fade on the* SECOND NURSE)

SCENE SIX

NURSE

Well, how is the Great White Doctor this evening?

INTERN (*Irritable*)

Oh . . . drop it.

NURSE

Oh, my . . . where is your cheerful demeanor this evening, Doctor?

INTERN

(*Smiling in spite of himself*) How do you do it? How do you manage to just dismiss things from your mind? How can you say a . . . cheerful hello to someone . . . dismissing from your mind . . . excusing yourself for the vile things you have said the evening before?

NURSE (*Lightly*)

I said nothing vile. I put you in your place . . . that's all. I . . . I merely put you in your place . . . as I have done before . . . and as I shall do again.

INTERN

(*Is about to say something; thinks better of it; sighs*) Never mind . . . forget about it . . . Did you *see* the sunset?

NURSE (*Mimicking*)

No, I didn't *see* the sunset. *What* is it doing?

INTERN

(*Amused. Puts it on heavily*) The west is burning . . . fire has enveloped fully half of the continent . . . the . . . the fingers of the flame stretch upward to the stars . . . and . . . and there is a monstrous burning circumference hanging on the edge of the world.

NURSE (*Laughs*)
Oh, my . . . oh, my.

INTERN (*Serious*)
It's a truly beautiful sight. Go out and have a look.

NURSE (*Coquettish*)
Oh, Doctor, I am chained to my desk of pain, so I must
rely on you. . . . Talk the sunset to me, you . . . you
monstrous burning intern hanging on the edge of my
circumference . . . ha, ha, *ha*.

INTERN
(*Leans toward her*) When?

NURSE
When?

INTERN (*Lightly*)
When . . . when are you going to let me nearer, woman?

NURSE
Oh, my!

INTERN
Here am I . . . here am I tangential, while all the while I
would serve more nobly as a radiant, not outward from,
but reversed, plunging straight to your lovely vortex.

NURSE (*Laughs*)

Oh, la! You must keep your mind off my lovely vortex
. . . you just remain . . . uh . . . tangential.

INTERN (*Mock despair*)

How is a man to fulfill himself? Here I offer you love . . .
consider the word . . . love. . . . Here I offer you my
love, my self . . . my bored bed . . .

NURSE

I note your offer . . . your offer is noted. (*Holds out a
clip board*) Here . . . do you want your reports?

INTERN

No . . . I don't want my reports. Give them here. (*Takes
the clip board*)

NURSE

And while you're here with your hot breath on me, hand
me a cigarette. I sent the nigger down for a pack. I ran
out. (*He gives her a cigarette*) Match?

INTERN

Go light it on the sunset. (*Tosses match to her*) He says
you owe him for three packs.

NURSE

(*Lights her cigarette*) Your bored bed . . . indeed.

INTERN

Ma'am . . . the heart yearns, the body burns . . .

NURSE

And *I* haven't time for *in*terns.

INTERN

. . . the heart yearns, the body burns . . . and I haven't
time . . . Oh, I don't know . . . the things you women
can do to art.
(*More intimate, but still light*)
Have you told your father, yet? Have you told your father
that I am hopelessly in love with you? Have you told him
that at night the sheets of my bed are like a tent, poled
center-upward in my love for you?

NURSE (*Wry*)

I'll tell him . . . I'll tell my father just that . . . just
what you said . . . and he'll be down here after you for
talking to a young lady like that! Really!

INTERN

My God! I forgot myself! A cloistered maiden in whose
house trousers are never mentioned . . . in which flies, I
am sure, are referred to only as winged bugs. Here I
thought I was talking to someone, to a certain young nurse,
whose collection of anatomical jokes for all occasions . . .

NURSE (*Giggles*)

Oh, you be still, now. (*Lofty*) Besides, just because I play coarse and flip around here . . . to keep my place with the rest of you . . . don't you think for a minute that I relish this turn to the particular from the general. . . . If you don't mind, we'll just cease this talk.

INTERN (*Half sung*)

I'm always in tumescence for you. You'd never guess the things I . . .

NURSE (*Blush-giggle*)

Now stop that! Really, I mean it!

INTERN

Then marry me, woman. If nothing else, marry me.

NURSE

Don't, now.

INTERN

(*Joking and serious at the same time*) Marry me.

NURSE

(*Matter-of-fact, but not unkindly*) I am sick of this talk. My poor father may have some funny ideas; he may be having a pretty hard time reconciling himself to things as they are. But not me! Forty-six dollars a month! Isn't that right? Isn't that what you make? Forty-six dollars a month!

Boy, you can't afford even to think about marrying. You can't afford marriage. . . . Best you can afford is lust. That's the best you can afford.

INTERN (*Scathing*)

Oh . . . gentle woman . . . nineteenth-century lady out of place in this vulgar time . . . maiden versed in petit point and murmured talk of the weather . . .

NURSE

Now I mean it . . . you can cut that talk right out.

INTERN

. . . type my great-grandfather fought and died for . . . forty-six dollars a month and the best I can afford is lust! Jesus, woman!

NURSE

All right . . . you can quit making fun of me. You can quit it right this minute.

INTERN

I! Making fun of *you* . . . !

NURSE

I am tired of being toyed with; I am tired of your impractical propositions. Must you dwell on what is not going to happen? Must you ask me, constantly, over and over again, the same question to which you are already

104

aware you will get the same answer? Do you get pleasure from it? What unreasonable form of contentment do you derive from persisting in this?

INTERN (*Lightly*)

Because I love you?

NURSE

Oh, that would help matters along; it really would . . . even if it were *true*. The economic realities would pick up their skirts, whoop, and depart before the lance-high, love-smit knight. My knight, whose real and true interest, if we come right down to it, as indicated in the order of your propositions, is, and always has been, a convenient and un-complicated bedding down.

INTERN

(*Smiling, and with great gallantry*) I have offered to marry you.

NURSE

Yeah . . . sure . . . you have offered to marry me. The United States is chuck-full of girls who have heard that great promise—I will marry you . . . I will marry you . . . IF! If! The great promise with its great conditional attached to it. . . .

INTERN (*Amused*)

Who are you pretending to be?

105

NURSE (*Abrupt*)
What do you mean?

INTERN (*Laughing*)
Oh, *nothing.*

NURSE
(*Regards him silently for a moment; then*) Marry me! Do
you know . . . do you know that nigger I sent to fetch me
a pack of butts . . . do you know he is in a far better
position . . . realistically, economically . . . to ask to
marry me than you are? Hunh? Do you know that? That
nigger! Do you know that nigger outearns you . . . and
by a *lot?*

INTERN
(*Bows to her*) I know he does . . . and I know what
value you, you and your famous family, put on such things.
So, I have an idea for you . . . why don't you just *ask*
that nigger to marry you? 'Cause, boy, he'd never ask you!
I'm sure if you told your father about it, it would give
him some pause at first, because we know what type of
man your father is . . . don't we? . . . But then he
would think about it . . . and realize the advantages of
the match . . . realistically . . . economically . . . and
he would find some way to adjust his values, in considera-
tion of your happiness, and security. . . .

NURSE

(*Flicks her still-lit cigarette at him, hard; hits him with it*)
You are disgusting!

INTERN

Damn you, bitch!

NURSE

Disgusting!

INTERN

Realistic . . . practical . . . (*A little softer, now*) Your
family is a famous *name*, but those thousand acres are *gone*,
and the pillars of your house are blistered and flaking . . .
(*Harder*) Not that your family ever *had*, within human
memory, a thousand acres to *go* . . . *or* a house with
pillars in the first place. . . .

NURSE (*Angry*)

I am fully aware of what is true and what is not true.
(*Soberly*) Go about your work and leave me be.

INTERN (*Sweetly*)

Aw.

NURSE

I said . . . leave me be.

107

INTERN

(*Brushing himself*) It is a criminal offense to set fire to interns . . . orderlies you may burn at will, unless you have other plans for them . . . but interns . . .

NURSE

. . . are a dime a dozen. (*Giggles*) Did I burn you?

INTERN

No, you did not burn me.

NURSE

That's too bad . . . would have served you right if I had. (*Pauses; then smiles*) I'm sorry, honey.

INTERN (*Mock formal*)

I accept your apology . . . and I await your surrender.

NURSE (*Laughs*)

Well, you just await it. (*A pause*) Hey, what are you going to do about the mayor being here now?

INTERN

What am I supposed to do about it? I am on emergencies, and he is not an emergency case.

NURSE

I told you . . . I told you what you should do.

INTERN

I know . . . I should go upstairs to his room . . . I should pull up a chair, and I should sit down and I should say, How's tricks, Your Honor?

NURSE

Well, you make fun if you want to . . . but if you listen to me, you'll know you need some people *behind* you.

INTERN

Strangers!

NURSE

Strangers don't stay strangers . . . not if you don't let them. He could do something for you if he had a mind to.

INTERN

Yes he could . . . indeed, he *could* do something for me. . . . He could give me his car . . . he could make me a present of his Cord automobile. . . . That would be the finest thing any mayor ever did for a private citizen. Have you seen that car?

NURSE

Have I seen that car? Have I seen this . . . have I seen that? Cord automobiles and . . . and sunsets . . . those are . . . fine preoccupations. Is that what you think about? Huh? Driving a fine car into a fine sunset?

INTERN (*Quietly*)
Lord knows, I'd like to get away from here.

NURSE (*Nodding*)
I know . . . I know. Well, maybe you're going to *have* to
get away from here. People are aware how dissatisfied you
are . . . people have heard a lot about your . . . dissatisfactions. . . . My father has heard . . . people got wind
of the way you feel about things. People here aren't good
enough for your attentions. . . . Foreigners . . . a bunch
of foreigners who are cutting each other up in their own
business . . . that's where you'd like to be, isn't it?

INTERN (*Quietly; intensely*)
There are over half a million people killed in that war! Do
you know that? By airplanes. . . . Civilians! You misunderstand me so! I am . . . all right . . . this way. . . .
My dissatisfactions . . . you call them that . . . my dissatisfactions have nothing to do with loyalties. . . . I am
not concerned with politics . . . but I have a sense of
urgency . . . a dislike of waste . . . stagnation . . . I am
stranded . . . *here.* . . . My talents are not large . . .
but the emergencies of the emergency ward of this second-
rate hospital in this second-rate state . . . No! . . . it isn't
enough. Oh, you listen to me. If I could . . . if I could
bandage the arm of one person . . . if I could be over
there right this minute . . . you could take the city of
Memphis . . . you could take the whole state . . . and

don't you forget I was born here . . . you could take the
whole goddam state. . . .

NURSE (*Hard*)

Well, I have a very good idea of how we could arrange
that. I have a dandy idea. . . . We could just tell the
mayor about the way you feel, and he'd be delighted to
help you on your way . . . out of this hospital at the very
least, and maybe out of the state! And I don't think he'd
be giving you any Cord automobile as a going-away
present, either. He'd set you out, all right . . . he'd set
you right out on your *butt!* That's what he'd do.

INTERN

(*With a rueful half-smile*) Yes . . . yes . . . I imagine he
would. I feel lucky . . . I feel doubly fortunate, now . . .
having you . . . feeling the way we do about each other.

NURSE

You are so sarcastic!

INTERN

Well, how the hell do you expect me to behave?

NURSE

Just . . . (*Laughs*) . . . oh, boy, this is good . . . just
like I told the nigger . . . you walk a straight line, and
you do your job . . . (*Turns coy, here*) . . . and . . .
and unless you are kept late by some emergency more

111

pressing than your . . . (*Smiles wryly*) . . . "love" . . .
for me . . . I may let you drive me home tonight . . . in
your beat-up Chevvy.

INTERN

Woman, as always I anticipate with enormous pleasure the
prospect of driving you home . . . a stop along the way
. . . fifteen minutes or so of . . . of tantalizing prelimin-
ary love play ending in an infuriating and inconclusive
wrestling match, during which you hiss of the . . . the
liberties I should not take, and I sound the horn once or
twice accidentally with my elbow . . .
    (*She giggles at this*)
. . . and, finally, in my beat-up car, in front of your
father's beat-up house . . . a kiss of searing intensity . . .
a hand in the right place . . . briefly . . . and your hasty
departure within. I am looking forward to this ritual . . .
as I always do.

NURSE (*Pleased*)

Why, thank you.

INTERN

I look forward to this ritual because of how it sets me
apart from other men . . .

NURSE

Aw . . .

INTERN

. . . because I am probably the only white man under sixty in two counties who has *not* had the pleasure of . . .

NURSE

LIAR! You no-account mother-grabbing son of a nigger!

INTERN (*Laughs*)

Boy! Watch you go!

NURSE

FILTH! You are filth!

INTERN

I am honest . . . an honest man. Let me make you an honest woman.

NURSE

(*Steaming . . . her rage between her teeth*) You have done it, boy . . . you have played around with me and you have done it. I am going to get you . . . I am going to fix you . . . I am going to see to it that you are *through* here . . . do you understand what I'm telling you?

INTERN

There is no ambiguity in your talk now, honey.

113

NURSE

You're damn right there isn't.
>   (*The* ORDERLY *re-enters from stage-rear. The* NURSE
>   *sees him*)

Get out of here!
>   (*But he stands there*)

Do you hear me? You get the hell out of here! GO!
>   (*He retreats, exits, to silence*)

INTERN (*Chuckling*)

King of the castle. My, you *are* something.

NURSE

Did you get what I was telling you?

INTERN

Why, I heard every word . . . every sweet syllable. . . .

NURSE

You have overstepped yourself . . . and you are going to
wish you hadn't. I'll get my father . . . I'll have you done
with *myself.*

INTERN (*Cautious*)

Aw, come on, now.

NURSE

I mean it.

INTERN (*Lying badly*)
Now look . . . you don't think I meant . . .

NURSE (*Mimicking*)
Now you don't think I meant . . . (*Laughs broadly*) Oh,
my . . . you are the funny one.
>   (*Her threat, now, has no fury, but is filled with
>   quiet conviction*)

I said I'll fix you . . . and I will. You just go along with
your work . . . you do your job . . . but what I said
. . . you keep that burning in the back of your brain.
We'll go right along, you and I, and we'll be civil . . .
and it'll be as though nothing had happened . . . nothing
at all. (*Laughs again*) Honey, your neck is in the *noose*
. . . and I have a whip . . . and I'll set the horse from
under you . . . when it pleases me.

INTERN (*Wryly*)
It's going to be nice around here.

NURSE
Oh, yes it is. I'm going to enjoy it . . . I really am.

INTERN
Well . . . I'll forget about driving you home tonight. . . .

NURSE
Oh, no . . . you will *not* forget about driving me home
tonight. You will drive me home *tonight* . . . you will

drive me home *tonight* . . . and *tomorrow* night . . . you will see me to my *door* . . . you will be my gallant. We will have things between us a little bit the way I am told things *used* to be. You will *court* me, boy, and you will do it *right!*

INTERN

(*Stares at her for a moment*) You impress me. No matter what else, I've got to admit that.
(*The* NURSE *laughs wildly at this.*
Music.
The lights on this hospital set fade, and come up on the SECOND NURSE, *at her desk, for*)

SCENE SEVEN

JACK

(*Rushing in*) Ma'am, I need help, quick!

SECOND NURSE

What d'you want here?

JACK

There has been an accident, ma'am . . . I got an injured woman outside in my car. . . .

SECOND NURSE

Yeah? Is that so? Well, you sit down and wait. . . . You go over there and sit down and wait a while.

JACK

This is an emergency! There has been an accident!

SECOND NURSE

YOU WAIT! You just sit down and wait!

JACK

This woman is badly hurt. . . .

SECOND NURSE

YOU COOL YOUR HEELS!

JACK

Ma'am . . . I got Bessie Smith out in that car there. . . .

SECOND NURSE

I DON'T CARE WHO YOU GOT OUT THERE, NIGGER. YOU COOL YOUR HEELS!
(*Music up.*
The lights fade on this scene, come up again on the main hospital scene, on the NURSE *and the* INTERN, *for*)

SCENE EIGHT

(*Music fades*)

NURSE (*Loud*)

Hey, nigger . . . nigger!
(*The* ORDERLY *re-enters*)
Give me my cigarettes.

117

INTERN

I think I'll . . .

NURSE

You stay here!
　　(*The* ORDERLY *hands the nurse the cigarettes, cautious and attentive to see what is wrong*)
A person could die for a smoke, the time you take. What'd you do . . . sit downstairs in the can and rest your small, shapely feet . . . hunh?

ORDERLY

You told me to . . . go back outside . . .

NURSE

Before that! What'd you do . . . go to the cigarette *factory?* Did you take a quick run up to Winston-Salem for these?

ORDERLY

No . . . I . . .

NURSE

Skip it. (*To the* INTERN) Where? Where were you planning to go?

INTERN (*Too formal*)

I beg your pardon?

118

NURSE

I said . . . where did you want to go to? Were you off for coffee?

INTERN

Is that what you want? Now that you have your cigarettes, have you hit upon the idea of having coffee, too? Now that he is back from one errand, are you planning to send me on another?

NURSE (*Smiling wickedly*)

Yeah . . . I think I'd like that . . . keep both of you jumping. I *would* like coffee, and I *would* like you to get it for me. So why don't you just trot right across the hall and get me some? And I like it good and hot . . . and strong . . .

INTERN

. . . and black . . . ?

NURSE

Cream! . . . and sweet . . . and in a hurry!

INTERN

I guess your wish is my command . . . hunh?

NURSE

You bet it is!

INTERN
(*Moves halfway to the door, stage-rear, then pauses*)
I just had a lovely thought . . . that maybe sometime
when you are sitting there at your desk opening mail with
that stiletto you use for a letter opener, you might slip and
tear open your arm . . . then you could come running
into the emergency . . . and I could be there when you
came running in, blood coming out of you like water out
of a faucet . . . and I could take ahold of your arm . . .
and just hold it . . . just hold it . . . and watch it flow
. . . just hold on to you and watch your blood flow. . . .

NURSE
(*Grabs up the letter opener . . . holds it up*)
This? More likely between your ribs!

INTERN (*Exiting*)
One coffee, lady.

NURSE
(*After a moment of silence, throws the letter opener
back down on her desk*)
I'll take care of him. CRACK! I'll crack that whip. (*To
the* ORDERLY) What are you standing there for . . . hunh?
You like to watch what's going on?

ORDERLY
I'm no voyeur.

NURSE

You what? You like to listen in? You take pleasure in it?

ORDERLY

I said no.

NURSE (*Half to herself*)

I'll bet you don't. I'll take care of him . . . talking to me
like that . . . I'll crack that whip. Let him just wait.
(*To the* ORDERLY, *now*)
My father says that Francisco Franco is going to be
victorious in that war over there . . . that he's going to
win . . . and that it's just wonderful.

ORDERLY

He does?

NURSE

Yes, he does. My father says that Francisco Franco has got
them licked, and that they're a bunch of radicals, anyway,
and it's all to the good . . . just wonderful.

ORDERLY

Is that so?

NURSE

I've told you my father is a . . . a historian, so he isn't
just anybody. His opinion counts for something special.

121

It *still* counts for something special. He says anybody wants to go over there and get mixed up in that thing has got it coming to him . . . whatever happens.

ORDERLY

I'm sure your father is an informed man, and . . .

NURSE

What?

ORDERLY

I said . . . I said . . . I'm sure your father is an informed man, and . . . his opinion is to be respected.

NURSE

That's right, boy . . . you just jump to it and say what you think people want to hear . . . you be both sides of the coin. Did you . . . did you hear him threaten me there? Did you?

ORDERLY

Oh, now . . . I don't think . . .

NURSE (*Steely*)

You heard him threaten me!

ORDERLY

I don't think . . .

NURSE

For such a smart boy . . . you are so dumb. I don't know what I am going to do with you.

> (*She is thinking of the* INTERN *now, and her expression shows it*)

You refuse to comprehend things, and that bodes badly . . . it does. Especially considering it is all but arranged . . .

ORDERLY

What is all but arranged?

NURSE

> (*A great laugh, but mirthless. She is barely under control*)

Why, don't you know, boy? Didn't you know that you and I are practically engaged?

ORDERLY

I . . . I don't . . .

NURSE

Don't you know about the economic realities? Haven't you been appraised of the way things *are?* (*She giggles*) Our knights are gone forth into sunsets . . . behind the wheels of Cord cars . . . the acres have diminished and the paint is flaking . . . that there is a great . . . *abandonment?*

123

ORDERLY (*Cautious*)

I don't understand you. . . .

NURSE

No kidding? (*Her voice shakes*) No kidding . . . you
don't understand me? Why? What's the matter, boy, don't
you get the idea?

ORDERLY (*Contained, but angry*)

I think you'd tire of riding me some day. I think you
would. . . .

NURSE

You go up to Room 206, right now . . . you go up and
tell the mayor that when his butt's better we have a marrying job for him.

ORDERLY (*With some distaste*)

Really . . . you go much too far. . . .

NURSE

Oh, I do, do I? Well, let me tell you something . . . I
am sick of it! I am *sick*. I am sick of everything in this hot,
stupid, fly-ridden *world*. I am sick of the disparity between
things as they are, and as they should be! I am sick of this
desk . . . this uniform . . . it scratches. . . . I am sick
of the sight of *you* . . . the *thought* of you makes me
. . . *itch*. . . . I am sick of *him*. (*Soft now: a chant*) I

am sick of talking to people on the phone in this damn stupid hospital. . . . I am sick of the smell of Lysol . . . I could die of it. . . . I am sick of going to bed and I am sick of waking up. . . . I am tired . . . I am tired of the truth . . . and I am tired of lying about the truth . . . I am tired of my skin. . . . I WANT OUT!

ORDERLY

(*After a short pause*) Why don't you go into emergency . . . and lie down?
    (*He approaches her*)

NURSE

Keep away from me.
    (*At this moment the outside door bursts open and* JACK *plunges into the room. He is all these things: drunk, shocked, frightened. His face should be cut, but no longer bleeding. His clothes should be dirtied . . . and in some disarray. He pauses, a few steps into the room, breathing hard*)

NURSE

Whoa! Hold on there, you.

ORDERLY (*Not advancing*)

What do you want?

JACK

(*After more hard breathing; confused*) What . . . ?

NURSE

You come banging in through that door like that? What's the matter with you? (*To the* ORDERLY) Go see what's the matter with him.

ORDERLY (*Advancing slightly*)

What do you *want?*

JACK (*Very confused*)

What do I want . . . ?

ORDERLY (*Backing off*)

You can't come in here like this . . . banging your way in here . . . don't you know any better?

NURSE

You drunk?

JACK

(*Taken aback by the irrelevance*) I've been drinking . . . yes . . . all right . . . I'm drunk. (*Intense*) I got someone outside . . .

NURSE

You stop that yelling. This is a white hospital, you.

ORDERLY (*Nearer the* NURSE)

That's right. She's right. This is a private hospital . . . a semiprivate hospital. If you go on . . . into the city . . .

JACK (*Shakes his head*)

No. . . .

NURSE

Now you listen to me, and you get this straight . . . (*Pauses just perceptibly, then says the word, but with no special emphasis*) . . . nigger . . . this is a semiprivate white hospital . . .

JACK (*Defiant*)

I don't care!

NURSE

Well, you *get* on. . . .

ORDERLY

(*As the* INTERN *re-enters with two containers of coffee*)

You go on now . . . you go . . .

INTERN

What's all this about?

ORDERLY

I told him to go on into Memphis . . .

INTERN

Be quiet. (*To* JACK) What is all this about?

JACK

Please . . . I got a woman . . .

NURSE

You been told to move on.

INTERN

You got a woman . . .

JACK

Outside . . . in the car. . . . There was an accident . . .
there is blood. . . . Her arm . . .

INTERN

(*After thinking for a moment, looking at the* NURSE,
moves toward the outside door)
All right . . . we'll go see. (*To the* ORDERLY, *who hangs
back*) Come on, you . . . let's go.

ORDERLY

(*Looks to the* NURSE) We told him to go on into Memphis.

NURSE

(*To the* INTERN, *her eyes narrowing*) Don't you go out
there!

INTERN

(*Ignoring her; to the* ORDERLY) You heard me . . . come
on!

128

NURSE (*Strong*)

I told you . . . DON'T GO OUT THERE!

INTERN (*Softly, sadly*)

Honey . . . you going to fix me? You going to have the mayor throw me out of here on my butt? Or are you going to arrange it in Washington to have me *deported?* What *are* you going to do . . . hunh?

NURSE (*Between her teeth*)

Don't go out there. . . .

INTERN

Well, honey, whatever it is you're going to do . . . it might as well be now as any other time.

(*He and the* ORDERLY *move to the outside door*)

NURSE

(*Half angry, half plaintive, as they exit*)

Don't go!

(*After they exit*)

I warn you! I *will* fix you. You go out that door . . . you're through here.

(JACK *moves to a vacant area near the bench, stage-right. The* NURSE *lights a cigarette*)

I told you I'd fix you . . . I'll fix you. (*Now*, to JACK) I think I said this was a white hospital.

JACK (*Wearily*)

I know, lady . . . you told me.

NURSE

(*Her attention on the door*) You don't have sense enough to do what you're told . . . you make trouble for yourself . . . you make trouble for other people.

JACK (*Sighing*)

I don't care. . . .

NURSE

You'll care!

JACK

(*Softly, shaking his head*) No . . . I won't care. (*Now, half to her, half to himself*) We were driving along . . . not very fast . . . I don't think we were driving fast . . . we were in a hurry, yes . . . and I had been drinking . . . *we* had been drinking . . . but I *don't* think we were driving fast . . . not too fast . . .

NURSE

(*Her speeches now are soft comments on his*) . . . driving drunk on the road . . . it not even dark yet . . .

JACK

. . . but then there was a car . . . I hadn't seen it . . . it couldn't have seen me . . . from a side road . . . hard, fast, sudden . . . (*Stiffens*) . . . *CRASH!* (*Loosens*) . . . and we weren't thrown . . . both of us . . . both cars stayed on the road . . . but we were stopped . . . my motor, running. . . . I turned it off . . . the door . . . the right door was all smashed in. . . . That's all it was . . . no more damage than that . . . but we had been riding along . . . laughing . . . it was cool driving, but it was warm out . . . and she had her arm out the window . . .

NURSE

. . . serves you right . . . drinking on the road . . .

JACK

. . . and I said . . . I said, Honey, we have crashed . . . you all right? (*His face contorts*) And I looked . . . and the door was all pushed in . . . she was caught there . . . where the door had pushed in . . . her right side, crushed into the torn door, the door crushed into her right side. . . . BESSIE! BESSIE! . . . (*More to the* NURSE, *now*) . . . but ma'am . . . her arm . . . her right arm . . . was torn off . . . almost torn off from her shoulder . . . and there was blood . . . SHE WAS BLEEDING SO . . . !

NURSE (*From a distance*)

Like water from a faucet . . . ? Oh, that is terrible . . . terrible. . . .

JACK

I didn't wait for nothin' . . . the other people . . . the other car . . . I started up . . . I started . . .

NURSE (*More alert*)

You took *off?* . . . You took off from an accident?

JACK

Her arm, ma'am . . .

NURSE

You probably got police looking for you right now . . . you know that?

JACK

Yes, ma'am . . . I suppose so . . . and I drove . . . there was a hospital about a mile up . . .

NURSE

(*Snapping to attention*) THERE! You went somewhere *else?* You been somewhere else already? What are you doing *here* with that woman then, hunh?

JACK

At the hospital . . . I came in to the desk and I told them

what had happened . . . and they said, you sit down and
wait . . . you go over there and sit down and wait a while.
WAIT! It was a white hospital, ma'am . . .

NURSE

This is a white hospital, too.

JACK

I said . . . this is an emergency . . . there has been an
accident. . . . YOU WAIT! You just sit down and wait.
. . . I told them . . . I told them it was an emergency
. . . I said . . . this woman is badly hurt. . . . YOU
COOL YOUR HEELS! . . . I said, Ma'am, I got Bessie
Smith out in that car there. . . . I DON'T CARE WHO
YOU GOT OUT THERE, NIGGER . . . YOU
COOL YOUR HEELS! . . . I couldn't wait there . . .
her in the car . . . so I left there . . . I drove on . . . I
stopped on the road and I was told where to come . . .
and I came here.

NURSE (*Numb, distant*)

I know who she is . . . I heard her sing. (*Abruptly*) You
give me your name! You can't take off from an accident
like that . . . I'll phone the police; I'll tell them where
you are!

> (*The* INTERN *and the* ORDERLY *re-enter. Their uni-
> forms are bloodied. The* ORDERLY *moves stage-rear,
> avoiding* JACK. *The* INTERN *moves in, staring at*
> JACK)

NURSE

He drove away from an accident . . . he just took off
. . . and he didn't come right here, either . . . he's been
to one hospital *already*. I *warned* you not to get mixed up
in this. . . .

INTERN (*Softly*)

Shut up!
      (*Moves toward* JACK, *stops in front of him*)
You tell me something . . .

NURSE

I warned you! You didn't listen to me . . .

JACK

You want my name, too . . . is that what you want?

INTERN

No, that's not what I want.
      (*He is contained, but there is a violent emotion in-
      side him*)
You tell me something. When you brought her here . . .

JACK

I brought her here. . . . They wouldn't help her. . . .

INTERN

All right. When you brought her here . . . when you
brought this woman *here* . . .

NURSE

Oh, this is no plain woman . . . this is no ordinary nigger . . . this is Bessie Smith!

INTERN

When you brought this woman *here* . . . when you drove up *here* . . . when you brought this woman *here* . . . DID YOU KNOW SHE WAS DEAD?
     (*Pause*)

NURSE

Dead! . . . This nigger brought a dead woman here?

INTERN

(*Afraid of the answer*) Well . . . ?

NURSE (*Distantly*)

Dead . . . dead.

JACK

(*Wearily; turning, moving toward the outside door*) Yes . . . I knew she was dead. She died on the way here.

NURSE

(*Snapping to*) Where you going? Where do you think you're going? I'm going to get the police here for you!

JACK

     (*At the door*)
Just outside.

INTERN

(*As* JACK *exits*)
WHAT DID YOU EXPECT *ME* TO DO, EH? WHAT
WAS *I* SUPPOSED TO *DO?*
(JACK *pauses for a moment, looks at him blankly,
closes the door behind him*)
TELL ME! WHAT WAS I SUPPOSED TO DO?

NURSE (*Slyly*)

Maybe . . . maybe he thought you'd bring her back to
life . . . great white doctor. (*Her laughter begins now,
mounts to hysteria*) Great . . . white . . . doctor. . . .
Where are you going to go now . . . great . . . white
. . . doctor? You are finished. You have had your last
patient here. . . . Off you go, boy! You have had your
last patient . . . a nigger . . . a dead nigger lady . . .
WHO SINGS. Well . . . I sing, too, boy . . . I sing real
good. You want to hear me sing? Hunh? You want to
hear the way I sing? HUNH?
(*Here she begins to sing and laugh at the same time.
The singing is tuneless, almost keening, and the
laughter is almost crying*)

INTERN

(*Moves to her*)
Stop that! Stop that!
(*But she can't. Finally he slaps her hard across the
face. Silence. She is frozen, with her hand to her
face where he hit her. He backs toward the rear
door*)

136

ORDERLY
(*His back to the wall*)
I never heard of such a thing . . . bringing a dead woman here like that. . . . I don't know what people can be thinking of sometimes. . . .

(*The* INTERN *exits. The room fades into silhouette again. . . . The great sunset blazes; music up*)

CURTAIN

The Sandbox (1959)

A BRIEF PLAY, IN MEMORY OF MY GRANDMOTHER (1876-1959)

Music by William Flanagan

F<small>IRST</small> P<small>ERFORMANCE</small>: April 15, 1960. New York City.

The Jazz Gallery.

The Sandbox

The Players:

THE YOUNG MAN	.... 25.	A good-looking, well-built boy in a bathing suit.
MOMMY	.... 55.	A well-dressed, imposing woman.
DADDY	.... 60.	A small man; gray, thin.
GRANDMA	.... 86.	A tiny, wizened woman with bright eyes.
THE MUSICIAN	....	No particular age, but young would be nice.

Note:

When, in the course of the play, MOMMY and DADDY call each other by these names, there should be no suggestion of regionalism. These names are of empty affection and point up the pre-senility and vacuity of their characters.

The Scene:

A bare stage, with only the following: Near the footlights, far stage-right, two simple chairs set side by side, facing the audience; near the footlights, far stage-left, a chair facing stage-right with a music stand before it; farther back, and stage-center, slightly elevated and raked, a large child's sandbox with a toy pail and shovel; the background is the sky, which alters from brightest day to deepest night.

At the beginning, it is brightest day; the YOUNG MAN is alone on stage, to the rear of the sandbox, and to one side. He is doing calesthenics; he does calesthenics until quite at the very end of the play. These calesthenics, employing the arms only, should suggest the beating and fluttering of wings. The YOUNG MAN is, after all, the Angel of Death.

MOMMY *and* DADDY *enter from stage-left,* MOMMY *first.*

MOMMY

(*Motioning to Daddy*) Well, here we are; this is the beach.

DADDY (*Whining*)

I'm cold.

MOMMY

(*Dismissing him with a little laugh*) Don't be silly; it's as warm as toast. Look at that nice young man over there: *he* doesn't think it's cold. (*Waves to the* YOUNG MAN) Hello.

YOUNG MAN
(*With an endearing smile*) Hi!

MOMMY (*Looking about*)
This will do perfectly . . . don't you think so, Daddy?
There's sand there . . . and the water beyond. What do
you think, Daddy?

DADDY (*Vaguely*)
Whatever you say, Mommy.

MOMMY
(*With the same little laugh*) Well, of course . . . whatever I say. Then, it's settled, is it?

DADDY (*Shrugs*)
She's *your* mother, not mine.

MOMMY
I know she's my mother. What do you take me for? (*A pause*) All right, now; let's get on with it. (*She shouts into the wings, stage-left*) You! Out there! You can come in now.

> (*The* MUSICIAN *enters, seats himself in the chair, stage-left, places music on the music stand, is ready to play.* MOMMY *nods approvingly*)

MOMMY
Very nice; very nice. Are you ready, Daddy? Let's go get Grandma.

DADDY

Whatever you say, Mommy.

MOMMY

(*Leading the way out, stage-left*) Of course, whatever I say. (*To the* MUSICIAN) You can begin now.

> (*The* MUSICIAN *begins playing;* MOMMY *and* DADDY *exit; the* MUSICIAN, *all the while playing, nods to the* YOUNG MAN)

YOUNG MAN

(*With the same endearing smile*) Hi!

> (*After a moment,* MOMMY *and* DADDY *re-enter, carrying* GRANDMA. *She is borne in by their hands under her armpits; she is quite rigid; her legs are drawn up; her feet do not touch the ground; the expression on her ancient face is that of puzzlement and fear*)

DADDY

Where do we put her?

MOMMY

(*The same little laugh*) Wherever I say, of course. Let me see . . . well . . . all right, over there . . . in the sand-box. (*Pause*) Well, what are you waiting for, Daddy? . . . The sandbox!

> (*Together they carry* GRANDMA *over to the sand-box and more or less dump her in*)

146

GRANDMA

(*Righting herself to a sitting position; her voice a cross between a baby's laugh and cry*) Ahhhhhh! Graaaaa!

DADDY (*Dusting himself*)

What do we do now?

MOMMY

(*To the* MUSICIAN) You can stop now.
        (*The* MUSICIAN *stops*)
(*Back to* DADDY) What do you mean, what do we do now?
We go over there and sit down, of course. (*To the* YOUNG MAN) Hello there.

YOUNG MAN

(*Again smiling*) Hi!
        (MOMMY *and* DADDY *move to the chairs, stage-right, and sit down. A pause*)

GRANDMA

(*Same as before*) Ahhhhhh! Ah-haaaaaa! Graaaaaa!

DADDY

Do you think . . . do you think she's . . . comfortable?

MOMMY (*Impatiently*)

How would I know?

DADDY

(*Pause*) What do we do now?

THE SANDBOX

MOMMY

(*As if remembering*) We . . . wait. We . . . sit here . . . and we wait . . . that's what we do.

DADDY

(*After a pause*) Shall we talk to each other?

MOMMY

(*With that little laugh; picking something off her dress*) Well, *you* can talk, if you want to . . . if you can think of anything to *say* . . . if you can think of anything *new*.

DADDY (*Thinks*)

No . . . I suppose not.

MOMMY

(*With a triumphant laugh*) Of course not!

GRANDMA

(*Banging the toy shovel against the pail*) Haaaaaa! Ah-haaaaaa!

MOMMY

(*Out over the audience*) Be quiet, Grandma . . . just be quiet, and wait.

      (GRANDMA *throws a shovelful of sand at* MOMMY)

MOMMY

(*Still out over the audience*) She's throwing sand at me!
You stop that, Grandma; you stop throwing sand at
Mommy! (*To* DADDY) She's throwing sand at me.

(DADDY *looks around at* GRANDMA, *who screams at
him*)

GRANDMA

GRAAAAAA!

MOMMY

Don't look at her. Just . . . sit here . . . be very still . . .
and wait. (*To the* MUSICIAN) You . . . uh . . . you go
ahead and do whatever it is you do.

(*The* MUSICIAN *plays*)

(MOMMY *and* DADDY *are fixed, staring out beyond
the audience.* GRANDMA *looks at them, looks at the*
MUSICIAN, *looks at the sandbox, throws down the
shovel*)

GRANDMA

Ah-haaaaaa! Graaaaaa! (*Looks for reaction; gets none.
Now . . . directly to the audience*) Honestly! What a
way to treat an old woman! Drag her out of the house . . .
stick her in a car . . . bring her out here from the city
. . . dump her in a pile of sand . . . and leave her here
to set. I'm eighty-six years old! I was married when I was
seventeen. To a farmer. He died when I was thirty. (*To
the* MUSICIAN) Will you stop that, please?

(*The* MUSICIAN *stops playing*)

THE SANDBOX

I'm a feeble old woman . . . how do you expect anybody to hear me over that peep! peep! peep! (*To herself*) There's no respect around here. (*To the* YOUNG MAN) There's no respect around here!

YOUNG MAN

(*Same smile*) Hi!

GRANDMA

(*After a pause, a mild double-take, continues, to the audience*) My husband died when I was thirty (*indicates* MOMMY), and I had to raise that big cow over there all by my lonesome. You can imagine what *that* was like. Lordy! (*To the* YOUNG MAN) Where'd they get *you?*

YOUNG MAN

Oh . . . I've been around for a while.

GRANDMA

I'll bet you have! Heh, heh, heh. Will you look at you!

YOUNG MAN

(*Flexing his muscles*) Isn't that something? (*Continues his calesthenics*)

GRANDMA

Boy, oh boy; I'll say. Pretty good.

YOUNG MAN (*Sweetly*)

I'll say.

150

GRANDMA

Where ya from?

YOUNG MAN

Southern California.

GRANDMA (*Nodding*)

Figgers; figgers. What's your name, honey?

YOUNG MAN

I don't know. . . .

GRANDMA

(*To the audience*) Bright, too!

YOUNG MAN

I mean . . . I mean, they haven't given me one yet . . . the studio . . .

GRANDMA

(*Giving him the once-over*) You don't say . . . you don't say. Well . . . uh, I've got to talk some more . . . don't you go 'way.

YOUNG MAN

Oh, no.

GRANDMA

(*Turning her attention back to the audience*) Fine; fine. (*Then, once more, back to the* YOUNG MAN) You're . . . you're an actor, hunh?

151

YOUNG MAN (*Beaming*)

Yes. I am.

GRANDMA

(*To the audience again; shrugs*) I'm smart that way. *Anyhow*, I had to raise . . . *that* over there all by my lonesome; and what's next to her there . . . that's what she married. Rich? I tell you . . . money, money, money. They took me off the *farm* . . . which was real decent of them . . . and they moved me into the big town house with *them* . . . fixed a nice place for me under the stove . . . gave me an army blanket . . . and my own dish . . . my very own dish! So, what have I got to complain about? Nothing, of course. I'm not complaining. (*She looks up at the sky, shouts to someone off stage*) Shouldn't it be getting dark now, dear?

> (*The lights dim; night comes on. The* MUSICIAN *begins to play; it becomes deepest night. There are spots on all the players, including the* YOUNG MAN, *who is, of course, continuing his calisthenics*)

DADDY (*Stirring*)

It's nighttime.

MOMMY

Shhhh. Be still . . . wait.

DADDY (*Whining*)

It's so hot.

152

MOMMY

Shhhhhh. Be still . . . wait.

GRANDMA

(*To herself*) That's better. Night. (*To the* MUSICIAN)
Honey, do you play all through this part?
          (*The* MUSICIAN *nods*)
Well, keep it nice and soft; that's a good boy.
          (*The* MUSICIAN *nods again; plays softly*)
That's nice.
          (*There is an off-stage rumble*)

DADDY (*Starting*)

What was that?

MOMMY

(*Beginning to weep*) It was nothing.

DADDY

It was . . . it was . . . thunder . . . or a wave breaking
. . . or something.

MOMMY

(*Whispering, through her tears*) It was an off-stage rumble
. . . and you know what *that* means. . . .

DADDY

I forget. . . .

MOMMY

(*Barely able to talk*) It means the time has come for poor Grandma . . . and I can't bear it!

DADDY (*Vacantly*)

I . . . I suppose you've got to be brave.

GRANDMA (*Mocking*)

That's right, kid; be brave. You'll bear up; you'll get over it.
(*Another off-stage rumble . . . louder*)

MOMMY

Ohhhhhhhhhh . . . poor Grandma . . . poor Grandma. . . .

GRANDMA (*To* MOMMY)

I'm fine! I'm all right! It hasn't happened yet!
(*A violent off-stage rumble. All the lights go out, save the spot on the* YOUNG MAN; *the* MUSICIAN *stops playing*)

MOMMY

Ohhhhhhhhhh. . . . Ohhhhhhhhhh. . . .

(*Silence*)

GRANDMA

Don't put the lights up yet . . . I'm not ready; I'm not quite ready. (*Silence*) All right, dear . . . I'm about done.

154

(The lights come up again, to brightest day; the MUSICIAN *begins to play.* GRANDMA *is discovered, still in the sandbox, lying on her side, propped up on an elbow, half covered, busily shoveling sand over herself)*

GRANDMA *(Muttering)*

I don't know how I'm supposed to do anything with this goddam toy shovel. . . .

DADDY

Mommy! It's daylight!

MOMMY *(Brightly)*

So it is! Well! Our long night is over. We must put away our tears, take off our mourning . . . and face the future. It's our duty.

GRANDMA

(Still shoveling; mimicking) . . . take off our mourning . . . face the future. . . . Lordy!

*(*MOMMY *and* DADDY *rise, stretch.* MOMMY *waves to the* YOUNG MAN*)*

YOUNG MAN

(With that smile) Hi!

*(*GRANDMA *plays dead. (!)* MOMMY *and* DADDY *go over to look at her; she is a little more than half buried in the sand; the toy shovel is in her hands, which are crossed on her breast)*

155

MOMMY

(*Before the sandbox; shaking her head*) Lovely! It's . . . it's hard to be sad . . . she looks . . . so happy. (*With pride and conviction*) It pays to do things well. (*To the* MUSICIAN) All right, you can stop now, if you want to. I mean, stay around for a swim, or something; it's all right with us. (*She sighs heavily*) Well, Daddy . . . off we go.

DADDY

Brave Mommy!

MOMMY

Brave Daddy!
    (*They exit, stage-left*)

GRANDMA

(*After they leave; lying quite still*) It pays to do things well. . . . Boy, oh boy! (*She tries to sit up*) . . . well, kids . . . (*but she finds she can't*) . . . I . . . I can't get up. I . . . I can't move. . . .
    (*The* YOUNG MAN *stops his calisthenics, nods to the* MUSICIAN, *walks over to* GRANDMA, *kneels down by the sandbox*)

GRANDMA

I . . . can't move. . . .

YOUNG MAN

Shhhhh . . . be very still. . . .

GRANDMA

I . . . I can't move. . . .

YOUNG MAN

Uh . . . ma'am; I . . . I have a line here.

GRANDMA

Oh, I'm sorry, sweetie; you go right ahead.

YOUNG MAN

I am . . . uh . . .

GRANDMA

Take your time, dear.

YOUNG MAN

(*Prepares; delivers the line like a real amateur*) I am the Angel of Death. I am . . . uh . . . I am come for you.

GRANDMA

What . . . wha . . . (*Then, with resignation*) . . . ohhhh . . . ohhhh, I see.

> (*The* YOUNG MAN *bends over, kisses* GRANDMA *gently on the forehead*)

GRANDMA

> (*Her eyes closed, her hands folded on her breast again, the shovel between her hands, a sweet smile on her face*)

Well . . . that was very nice, dear. . . .

157

YOUNG MAN

(*Still kneeling*) Shhhhhh . . . be still. . . .

GRANDMA

What I meant was . . . you did that very well, dear. . . .

YOUNG MAN (*Blushing*)

. . . oh . . .

GRANDMA

No; I mean it. You've got that . . . you've got a quality.

YOUNG MAN

(*With his endearing smile*) Oh . . . thank you; thank you very much . . . ma'am.

GRANDMA

(*Slowly; softly—as the* YOUNG MAN *puts his hands on top of* GRANDMA's) You're . . . you're welcome . . . dear.

(*Tableau. The* MUSICIAN *continues to play as the curtain slowly comes down*)

CURTAIN